Interracial Bonds

RHODA GOLDSTEIN BLUMBERG
and WENDELL JAMES ROYE

GENERAL HALL, INC.
Publishers
23—45 Corporal Kennedy Street
Bayside, New York 11360

INTERRACIAL BONDS

Copyright © 1979 by General Hall, Inc.
All rights reserved, including the right to
reproduce this book, or parts thereof, in
any form, except for the inclusion of brief
quotations in a review.

ISBN: 0-930390-33-4 (paper)
      0-930390-34-2 (cloth)

Library of Congress Catalog Card Number: 79-63730
Manufactured in the United States of America

PREFACE

In our separate lives, one lived as a black man and the other as a white woman, we have experienced a variety of interracial contacts. We have been part of interracial teams and coalitions in academic and community settings. According to our observations, each as a university professor and Roye as a human relations specialist in private agencies, success came most often through cooperation that crossed racial and cultural lines. Our citizenship roles informed our intellectual understanding of intergroup relations processes. We found that, as people joined together with a shared instrumental purpose, that of achieving victory over racism, they frequently gained expressive rewards -- interracial friendships and mutual respect. Both knowledge and personal experience thus encouraged us to bring to others an exploration into the varieties of interracial bonds that are possible.

The initial idea for the book germinated in conversations between Blumberg and Helena Z. Lopata. Early encouragement was given by Robert Blauner and Alphonso Pinkney, both of whom saw a need for this type of work. When Roye agreed to co-edit, the project moved ahead. We thank those who gave support when needed, our contributors for their patience and cooperation, and Marion Hajdu for invaluable assistance in producing the manuscript.

R.G.B. and W.J.R.

FOR
Winston
and
Leah, Meyer and Helena

Contents

Preface		i
1.	Introduction by Rhoda Goldstein Blumberg	1
	PART I. A HISTORICAL CONTRAST	10
2.	The White Indians of Colonial America by James Axtell	11
3.	Bonds Between Indians and Other Racial Groups in an Urban Setting by C. Hoy Steele	36
	PART II. BONDS FOR EFFECTING POLITICAL AND SOCIAL ACTION	52
4.	Black and White Together: A Time to Remember by Priscilla Read Chenoweth	54
5.	Working Together for Social Change by Fred Cloud	63
6.	Twin-Track Coalitions in the Black Power Movement by Guida West	71
	PART III. BONDS THAT INTEGRATE	88
7.	When Integration Works by William Spinrad	89
8.	Creating Interracial Bonds in a Desegregated School by Janet Ward Schofield & Elaine Patricia McGivern	106
9.	Oreo--Marginal Man and Woman by Charles Vert Willie	120
	PART IV. PERSONAL BONDS	132
10.	Miss Anne and the Black Brother by June A. True	133
11.	Transracial Adoption: Can White Parents Bring Up a Healthy Black Child? by Joyce A. Ladner	153
12.	A Friendship: Part One by Gloria Feman Orenstein	175
	A Friendship: Part Two by Adah Askew	186
About the Authors		191
Index		196

1

INTRODUCTION

By

Rhoda Goldstein Blumberg

INTERRACIAL BONDS affirms a neglected, overlooked, and often discredited reality--positive interracial ties. The term refers to the variety of cooperative or friendly relationships, temporary or permanent, which develop or are consciously created when races and cultures meet. Bonds range from short-term coalitions for mutual advantage to intimate ties of friendship and love. They are sometimes forged in the heat of the persisting struggle against racial oppression. But others spring up as part of daily living: when neighbors become friends, when soldiers face danger together, when poor people struggle against shared misery, when a man and woman fall in love, when a white parent rears a black child.

In exploring this subject, through cases mostly representative of contemporary America, we depart from a central mood of writing in race relations. For the last decade and a half, black and third world writing has dramatically exposed the world-wide history and terror of European racism and domination over non-whites. The recurring themes of interracial violence, subjugation, colonialism and cruelty are now familiar in discourse about relationships between whites and those who are not white.

Why then a book on interracial bonds? Because throughout America's adversarial, multi-cultural history, there have been opposing trends: human relationships that have transcended color, colonizers who "refused" their roles, coalitions between unlikely partners, members of racial minorities who struggled against their historically validated mistrust of every white. This persistent, stubborn and ever-reemergent strand in race relations bears examination. Knowing that racism is used as a tool to divide those with common interests, it becomes ever more urgent to learn about instances in which racism can be transcended. We agree with Robin M. Williams, Jr., who states in his preface to *Mutual Accommodation: Ethnic Conflict and Cooperation:*

> To overlook or persistently minimize positively valued outcomes of relationships among ethnic groupings leaves us without models from which to learn practicable methods of constructive action....The simple logic of comparison suggests that we must pay greater attention to our successes-- recognize them, examine them, and find out why they worked.

There is probably no such thing as a "balanced" picture of the variety of interracial bonds. Most racial theory in the United States deals with the historical situation emanating out of slavery--the black-white relationship. Our book, too, follows this pattern. Contributions about interracial bonds other than those between blacks and whites were sought without much success. Minority and majority peoples are at different stages in their relationships with each other and among themselves.

Regardless of one's political viewpoint, the historical moment itself has much to do with whether or not members of different racial groups can work together, or write about positive interracial experiences. Joint action for social change, however, is neither radical nor liberal in itself and, while the labelling differs, finds validation under varied philosophical guises.

In presenting their views, most of the authors--whether academicians or activists--draw upon their own experiences in politics, social movements and personal life. They are far from naive about the perils involved in crossing racial lines, either in politics or social relationships. Many of the articles openly discuss these difficulties. Nonetheless, each author approached the task of writing an original essay out of the conviction that there was something that had to be said. A variety of styles will be evident: some sociological, some historical, and others biographical. Individual convictions differ, and represent only those of the writer. The white person who writes about interracial bonds may appear to be self-serving; the minority person, a compromiser. Rather than trying to eliminate totally any remark which might be construed as offensive--a task which probably would have proved impossible--the editors preferred to let each author's work stand on its own. Some of the selections are controversial and will, we believe, provoke lively classroom discussion and analysis.

To enhance readability, contributors were asked to minimize or eliminate footnotes. Only two selections were not written expressly for this book. Having seen James Axtell's "The White Indians of Colonial America," we felt that it clearly belonged in this collection. It is used in Part One to help the reader start with a historical perspective, and is followed by C. Hoy Steele's analysis of a contemporary case of Native-American-white relations. Charles V. Willie's article on interracial conciliation in Part Three has also been published previously and is included because of its obvious appropriateness.

It should not be surprising that our central theme is neglected, overlooked and frequently discredited. Given America's history of racism, members of both the dominant group and of subordinate racial groups may wish to overlook positive bonds. For those who prefer an idealized picture of American democracy, it is better to ignore both the racism that permeates our history and the ever-present strand of resistance and opposition to it by both whites and racial minorities.

Writing in the *Black Scholar* (January-February 1975), Herbert Aptheker draws attention to the hidden history of anti-racist thought in the United States. Aptheker's credentials in black history enable him to reintroduce this topic in a black, change-oriented journal. We agree with him that American history is distorted when viewed as static and when whites are seen as monolithic. Aptheker maintains that white individuals resisted and wrote against racism from the colonial period on. Despite law and custom outlawing interracial bonding, love, empathy and joint action in the quest for racial justice occurred. Aptheker documents not only anti-racism and anti-slavery literature by whites, but also the presence of warm human sentiments between the races in marriages, long-time love relationships, and child-rearing.

There is no evidence of natural hostility between individuals of different racial backgrounds. But numerous betrayals, in which trust in whites was misplaced, makes members of racial minorities suspicious of white "friends." Native Americans sometimes welcomed the European strangers, only to become victims of the expansion of Europe and an ideology which justified political, economic, cultural, and psychological subjugation. Racism became institutionalized. Hence, consciously and unconsciously, as Robert Blauner has so cogently put it, the white person stands to gain from the oppression of other races. To be neutral is to accept passively the gains or losses which accrue from the accident of one's color. Some would say that such gains can only be temporary.

Even those whites who consider racist systems an affront to human dignity need to counterbalance, through personal effort, all the forces that make them into unwilling racists. They, too, are victims of a culture that speaks everywhere of "the rightness of whiteness." Media, the operation of the educational system, the housing system, the criminal justice system--all establish and maintain the white advantage and prolong the subjugation of people of color. Just as the black, Puerto Rican or Chicano victim of these forces must engage in consciousness-raising, so the white person whose basic sentiments oppose racism must carefully reflect upon its unconscious influences. In the continuing struggle, a well-meaning white may unwittingly do more harm than good-for instance, take on an inappropriate leadership role and attempt to speak for minorities who must speak for themselves.

Studies of biracial school situations have shown that unless usual socialization processes are counter-balanced, both white and black children will tend to share complementary expectations about their relative competence in classroom performance--what Elizabeth G.Cohen and others have called "interracial interaction disability." That is, both groups will tend to assume that whites can perform better in this situation. It is this kind of discovery that periodically discourages interracial cooperation and causes rejection of white allies.

And yet, the coalitions do begin again because new situations seem to require them. Our second section provides four examples of joint black and white efforts to effect social change.

The Civil Rights movement of the 1960's was one of those times in United States history when whites joined with blacks in the effort to eliminate segregation and to establish voting and employment rights. Organizations such as the Congress of Racial Equality, about which one of our authors writes, have undergone many transformations since that time. The failure of the Freedom

Democratic Party to gain legitimation in the 1964 Presidential primaries signalled an end to this major period of black-white political cooperation. For many, faith in changing mainstream institutions through legal processes and integration waned. Black mistrust of sympathetic whites surfaced openly. A white who, by siding with the stigmatized, comes to share in the stigma has always been somewhat suspect, just because the alliance is voluntary. The black power movement began, with black leadership and black culture gaining ascendancy.

Although integrated participation declined, some whites continued to play supportive roles. Perhaps one of the more visible of these support activities was the "twin-track coalitions" described by Guida West in Part II. The twin-tracks, which arose simultaneously in a number of cities, were uneasy coalitions of community black power organizations and white support groups. To prevent "interracial interaction disability," separate meetings were held. The unequal partnership was, as so many other events of that period, an attempt to reverse the usual pattern of white dominance.

The historian Benjamin Quarles, in *Blacks and John Brown,* ' demonstrates the unfailing admiration black people had for the white martyr, John Brown, both while he lived and after his death. The names of Michael Schwerner and Andrew Goodman, white victims of racist terror, are frequently alluded to by black leaders as martyrs of the civil rights period. Yet, even in death, the irony of racism bore its brunt. James Chaney, the black youth who died with them, was severely beaten and shot repeatedly, unlike his white companions. Civil rights workers noted how the death of the two whites drew disproportionate attention. Thus does joint black and white effort get contaminated by the larger environment.

The white supporter tends also to become a surrogate for the white society, as pointed out by Marx and Useem in an article published in the *Journal of Social Issues.* Data from several sources (including June True's article in this volume) suggest that this is less likely to be so in the case of white females than males. At any rate, interracial bonds are rarely untroubled.

Their recurrence, all the more then, demands attention. Despite great variation in duration and intensity, interracial bonds sometimes prove functional. Frequently, they are created in order to accomplish a specific instrumental goal, such as electing a particular candidate or getting legislation passed. Fred Cloud recounts strategies by which an official governmental agency and private community groups were able to complement each other's efforts in the field of human rights. A municipal human relations commission may exist as a mere gesture to appease minorities. However, it can become a community force if leadership recognizes its potentialities and limitations and carefully plans coalition efforts. Nationally, there are many such relations commissions of varying effectiveness.

Bonds developed in working together for social change may remain polite and transitory or become intense and close. When such closeness enhances the personal lives of the individuals involved, fostering individual growth, expressive needs are met. Priscilla Chenoweth's personal narrative recounts her journey from a relatively limited background to a rich human experience.

Our third section deals with the issue of integration in several basic institutional areas: housing, education, the military and sports. The goal of integration, during the Civil Rights era, was based on a set of premises which denied the possibility of a "separate but equal" existence for blacks and whites. Structural integration, the participation of minorities in mainstream institutions was the way to insure that all would obtain their fair share of society's goods and services. Thus, the instrumental purpose of integration was not friendship, nor close relationships, but rather the securing of rights. Among the basic targets of desegregation efforts were housing, education, and employment. Some progress was made in desegregating southern schools. But blacks who came to the North seeking work were unable to follow the European ethnic pattern of moving out of the center cities. Instead, they were locked into ghettos by highly effective private and public housing policies.

Desegregation has turned out to be an even more difficult process in the North than in the South. Integration has always been opposed by white segregationists, who believe the separation of the races to be necessary, useful and even sacred. In the North, more recently than the South, school desegregation has been the setting for bitter struggle, and the term "busing"-- a mode of conveying children to schools throughout our history--acquired the prefix "forced." White backlash, supported by two national administrations, reinforced the disillusion of many with integration efforts. Yet alternatives seemed few in number. Rarely publicized were cases of peaceful desegregation.

Contributors to the third part, "Bonds That Integrate" write of integration efforts in different ways. Sociologist William Spinrad analyzes several selected institutions, noting the key elements present in successful integration attempts. In the area of housing, one of the most resistant to change, there is persistent struggle to break down the institutional barriers that keep low income and minority people segregated in ghettos. A connection can be made between Spinrad's analysis of housing and the final article, which deals with the friendship of two women, one black and one Jewish, who met as neighbors in a New York housing cooperative. Observe that somewhat successfully integrated areas such as sports bear continued monitoring. Although blacks have entered commercial sports as players, the question of their representation in the ranks of managers and coaches must be addressed. Further, the need to infuse black culture into mainstream institutions was made clear by the black cultural revolution of the 1960's. Black power proponents insisted that black pride and black consciousness were necessary preconditions to successful integration. Supporting their position is Robert Newby's finding that a diminution of "interracial interaction disability" has occurred, related to renewed black pride. His post black-power studies of black school children record an improvement in their self-esteem and self-comparisons with whites.

Even when peacefully initiated, desegregation is but the beginning of progress toward integration. Hostile or even indifferent administration easily creates newly segregated tracts. Many problems and tensions must be faced and overcome by those who seek to develop bonds between formerly separated groups. Psychologist Janet Ward Schofield and sociologist Elaine Patricia McGivern present a case study of a relatively successful effort made by teachers in a desegregated school. These teachers facilitated the development of a positive, shared identity among black and white seventh-graders. In this case, extra-curricular activities provided the mechanism; in others, learning experiences may be structured to encourage interracial cooperation rather than rivalry.

Our final selection on integration provides a bridge to Part IV, Personal Bonds. Using his own experiences in a leadership role at an annual religious conference, sociologist Charles V. Willie offers a vivid illustration of the interrelationship between group integration and personal bonds. He shows that personal lives are affected by, but can, in turn, affect group settings.

Cultural and racial differences do not keep people permanently apart, and in Part IV we deal with interracial bonds in the personal sphere. All of us need other human beings and sometimes racial lines are crossed in meeting these needs. There are always those few who flaunt customs, family and safety for the sake of love relationships. Conflict itself, leading to more equalization of relationships, tends to bring dominants and minorities together in many new situations. And equal status relationships, where such truly occur, tend to break down racial barriers.

However, the personal sphere and personal needs may not correspond with group goals. Personal interracial ties occur within the broader context of one group's oppression of another and hence take on the appearance of collusion with "the enemy." The factor of race complicates love and friendship (elusive in any case) because of both the social and cultural milieu and group pressures specifically forbidding such relationships. Society's view includes many beliefs about the ulterior motives for interracial love liaisons. Indeed, as Cleveland Sellers and Robert Terrell point out, in *River of No Return,* black-white sexual relationships, deemed dangerous and divisive, were ultimately forbidden in the interracial social action organization, SNCC. We found an author, June True, who chose to tackle this troublesome subject.

A selection also examines the controversial question of transracial adoption. Among the issues involved is the concern over whether or not a white parent can fully prepare a black child to appreciate and assume his/her racial identity. Joyce Ladner has taken material from her book on the subject to provide an analysis of this debate.

Finally, we chose to conclude with an unusual situation of interracial bonding--that between a black woman and a white woman, Adah Askew and Gloria F. Orenstein. Such interracial friendship has been considered improbable; black women and white women are sometimes viewed as rivals and enemies. But personal experience can contradict stereotypes, and in this case it did.

SOURCES

Herbert Apthéker, "The History of Anti-Racism in the United States," *The Black Scholar,* 6 (January-February, 1975): 16-22.

Robert Blauner, *Racial Oppression in America,* New York: Harper and Row, 1972.

Elizabeth G. Cohen, "Interracial Interaction Disability," *Human Relations,* 25 (no. 1): 9-24.

Erving Goffman, *Stigma,* Englewood Cliffs, N. J.: Prentice-Hall, Inc., 1963.

Gary T. Marx, and Michael Useem, "Majority Involvement in Minority Movements: Civil Rights, Abolition, and Untouchability," *Journal of Social Issues,* 27: 81-104.

Robert Newby, *The Effect of Black Racial Consciousness on Race As A Diffuse Status Characteristic,* Paper presented at the Pacific Sociological Association Meetings, San Jose, California, March 29, 1974.

Benjamin Quarles, (ed.), *Blacks on John Brown,* Urbana, Illinois: University of Illinois Press, 1972.

Cleveland Sellers with Robert Terrell, *The River of No Return,* New York: William Morrow and Company, 1973.

Robert G. Weisbord and Arthur Stein, *Bittersweet Encounter,* New York: Shocken Books, 1970.

Robin M. Williams, Jr., *Mutual Accommodation: Ethnic Conflict and Cooperation,* Minneapolis: University of Minnesota Press, 1977.

INTRODUCTION TO PART ONE

A HISTORICAL CONTRAST

Two essays on Native Americans begin this volume. In the first, James Axtell reveals that many of those captured by Indian tribes in North America developed strong personal ties with their captors. Some, in fact, refused to be rescued--so much did they love the Indian way of life and the Indian families into which they had been adopted.

If any racial prejudice did exist on the part of the Native Americans or the integrated whites, it was dissipated by a careful resocialization process, in which Indian values took strong hold and in which the whites became true family members. Given relatively equal exposure, to what set of values would our contemporary "good American" drift today? The preliterate or the computerized industrial civilization with which we press and bind the world? One may never know. The value complex Axtell's subjects embraced would today compete with mass production, sophisticated media information management and pervasive conformity conditioning. The Indian family relationships would contend with a host of opponents ranging from pre-head start programs to easy credit, to welfare. Nor would the assault upon Indian tribal and family identity need be direct. The possibility is that our captive would yearn for home, yet remain unable to identify what or where "home" is. Or maybe not. The alienated segment of our youth who seek a more simple, natural and humanistic life might wish for a way to be adopted.

Today bonds between Indians and whites are extremely tenuous. C. Hoy Steele, an anthropologist, studied Indian-white relations in a contemporary urban setting. By this time the continuing history of broken treaties, land-theft and Indian impoverishment had left their mark. Indian people no longer welcomed whites into their community and rarely trusted them. Steele analyzes the attempts of some whites to prove friendship, and the reasons why some did manage to earn acceptance. When it does occur, acceptance is on an individual basis. We present this case study because it provides such a stark historical contrast to the earlier Indian-white relations described by Axtell.

2

THE WHITE INDIANS OF COLONIAL AMERICA*

By

James Axtell

The English, like their French rivals, began their colonizing ventures in North America with a sincere interest in converting the Indians to Christianity and civilization. Nearly all the colonial charters granted by the English monarchs in the seventeenth century assigned the wish to extend the Christian Church and to redeem savage souls as a principal, if not *the* principal, motive for colonization. This desire was grounded in a set of complementary beliefs about "savagism" and "civilization." First, the English held that the Indians, however benighted, were capable of conversion. "It is not the nature of men," they believed, "but the education of men, which make them barbarous and uncivill." Moreover, the English were confident that the Indians would want to be converted once they were exposed to the superior quality of English life.

The second article of the English faith followed from their fundamental belief in the superiority of civilization, namely, that no civilized person in possession of his faculties or free from undue restraint would choose to become an Indian. "For, easy and unconstrained as the savage life is," wrote the Reverend William Smith of Philadelphia, "certainly it could never be put in competition with the blessings of improved life and the light of religion, by any persons who have had the happiness of enjoying, and the capacity of discerning, them."

And yet, by the close of the colonial period, very few if any Indians had been transformed into "civilized" Englishmen. Most of the Indians who were educated by the English--some contemporaries thought *all* of them--returned to Indian society at the first opportunity to resume their Indian identities. On the other hand, large numbers of Englishmen had chosen to become Indians--by running away from colonial society to join Indian society, by not trying to escape after being captured, or by electing to remain with their Indian captors when treaties of peace periodically afforded them the opportunity to return home.

The story of the "white Indians" of colonial America is based upon two kinds of documentary sources. The first is official government and military records, which describe the numbers and circumstance of the white captives in Indian hands and the difficulties in dealing with those forcibly returned to white society. The second and larger group of sources consists of hundreds of captivity narratives--the Newberry Library (Chicago) collection numbers over a thousand titles--written either by the captives themselves upon their return, by friends who took down their words if they were unable to write finished prose, or by sensationalist hack-writers out to make a dollar. Needless to say, the efforts of the latter are largely devoid of value for the historian. But many narratives, while appeasing the appetite of a growing audience for Indian "thrillers," were also written by simple, honest people for the sole sake of memory or their families and contain much more truth than fiction. Some of the best of these narratives were never published until the late nineteenth or twentieth century in scholarly periodicals or small editions. In these relatively unadorned accounts can be found the largest quotient of verifiable truth about the making of the "white Indians."

Perhaps the first colonist to recognize the disparity between the English dream and the American reality was Cadwallader Colden, surveyor-general and member of the king's council of New York. In his *History of the Five Indian Nations of Canada*, published in London in 1747, Colden described the Albany peace treaty between the French and the Iroquois in 1699, when "few of (the French captives) could be persuaded to return" to Canada. Lest his readers attribute this unusual behavior to "the Hardships they had endured in their own Country, under a tyrannical Government and a barren Soil," he quickly added that "the *English* had as much Difficulty to persuade the People, that had been taken Prisoners by the *French Indians*, to leave the *Indian* Manner of living, though no People enjoy more Liberty, and live in greater Plenty, than the common Inhabitants of

New-York do." Colden, clearly amazed, elaborated:
> No Arguments, no Intreaties, nor Tears of their Friends and Relations, could persuade many of them to leave their new *Indian* Friends and Acquaintance(s); several of them that were by the Caressings of their Relations persuaded to come Home, in a little Time grew tired of our Manner of living, and run away again to the *Indians*, and ended their Days with them. On the other Hand, *Indian* Children have been carefully educated among the *English*, cloathed and taught, yet, I think, there is not one Instance, that any of these, after they had liberty to go among their own People, and were come to Age, would remain with the *English*, but returned to their own Nations, and became as fond of the *Indian* Manner of Life as those who knew nothing of a civilized Manner of living. What I now tell of Christian Prisoners among *Indians* (he concluded his history), relates not only to what happened at the Conclusion of this War, but has been found true on many other Occasions.

Colden was not alone. Six years later Benjamin Franklin wondered how it was that:
> When an Indian Child has been brought up among us, taught our language and habituated to our Customs, yet if he goes to see his relations and makes one Indian Ramble with them, there is no perswading him ever to return. But when white persons of either sex have been taken prisoners young by the Indians, and lived a while among them, tho' ransomed by their Friends, and treated with all imaginable tenderness to prevail with them to stay among the English, yet in a Short time they become disgusted with our manner of life, and the care and pains that are necessary to support it, and take the first good Opportunity of escaping again into the Woods, from whence there is no reclaiming them.

In short, "thousands of Europeans are Indians," as Hector de Crevecoeur put it, "and we have no examples of even one of those Aborigines having from choice become Europeans!"

The English captives who foiled their countrymen's civilized assumptions by becoming Indians differed little from the general colonial population when they were captured. According to over 100 captivity narratives, they were ordinary men, women, and children of yeoman stock, Protestants by faith, a variety of nationalities by birth, English by law, different from their countrymen only in their willingness to risk personal insecurity for the economic opportunities of the frontier. There was no discernible characteristic or pattern of characteristics that differentiated them from their captive neighbors who eventually rejected Indian life--with one exception. Most of the colonists captured by the Indians and adopted into Indian families were children of both sexes and young women, often the mothers of the captive children. They were, as one captivity narrative observed, the "weak and defenceless."

The Indians obviously chose their captives carefully so as to maximize the chances of acculturating them to Indian life. To judge by the results, their methods were hard to fault. Even when the English held the upper hand militarily, they were often embarrassed by the Indians' educational power.

The close of hostilities in Pennsylvania came in 1764 after Col. Henry Bouquet defeated the Indians near Bushy Run and imposed peace. By the articles of agreement reached in October, the Delawares, Shawnees, and Senecas were to deliver up "all the Prisoners in (their) Possession, without any Exception, Englishmen, Frenchmen, Women, and Children, whether adopted in your Tribes, married, or living amongst you, under any Denomination, or Pretence whatever." In the weeks that followed, Bouquet's troops, including "the Relations of (some of) the People (the Indians) have Massacred, or taken Prisoners," encamped on the Muskingum in the heart of the Ohio country to collect the captives. On November 12, 1764, at his camp on the Muskinghum, Colonel Bouquet lectured the Shawnees who had not delivered all their captives: "As you are now going to Collect all our *Flesh*, and *Blood*, . . . I desire that you will use them with Tenderness, and look upon them as Brothers, and no longer as Captives." The utter gratuitousness of his remark was reflected-- no doubt purposely--in the Shawnee speech when the Indians delivered their captives the following spring at Fort Pitt. "Father-- Here is your *Flesh*, and *Blood* . . . they have been all tied to us by Adoption, although we now deliver them up to you. We will always look upon them as Relations, whenever the *Great Spirit* is pleased that we may visit them . . . Father--we have taken as much Care of these Prisoners, as if they were (our) own Flesh, and blood; they are become unacquainted with your Customs, and manners, and therefore, Father we request you will use them tender, and kindly, which will be a means of inducing them to live contentedly with you."

The Indians spoke the truth and the English knew it. Three days after his speech to the Shawnees, Bouquet had advised Lt. Gov. Francis Fauquier of Virginia that the returning captives "ought to be treated by their Relations with Tenderness and Humanity, till Time and Reason make them forget their unnatural Attachments, but unless they are closely watch'd," he admitted, "they will certainly return to the Barbarians." And indeed they would have, for during a half-century of conflict captives had been returned who, like many of the Ohio prisoners, responded only to Indian names, spoke only Indian dialects, felt comfortable only in Indian clothes, and in general regarded their white saviors as barbarians and their deliverance as captivity. Had they not been compelled to return to English society by militarily enforced peace treaties, the ranks of the white Indians would have been greatly enlarged.

From the moment the Indians surrendered their English prisoners, the colonists faced a number of difficult problems. The first was the problem of getting the prisoners to remain with the English. When Bouquet sent the first group of restored captives to Fort Pitt, he ordered his officers there that "they are to be closely watched and well Secured" because "most of them, particularly those who have been a long time among the Indians, will take the first Opportunity to run away." The young children especially were "so completely savage that they were brought to the camp tied hand and foot." Fourteen-year-old John McCullough, who had lived with the Indians for "eight years, four months, and sixteen days" (by his parents' reckoning), had his legs tied "under the horses belly" and his arms tied behind his back with his father's garters, but to no avail. He escaped under the cover of night and returned to his Indian family for a year before he was finally carried to Fort Pitt under "strong guard." "Having been accustomed to look upon the Indians as the only connexions they had, having been tenderly treated by them, and speaking their language," explained the Reverend William Smith, the historian of Bouquet's expedition, "it is no wonder that (the children) considered their new state in the light of a captivity, and parted from the savages with tears."

Children were not the only reluctant freedmen. "Several women eloped in the night, and ran off to join their Indian friends." Among them undoubtedly were some of the English women who had married Indian men and borne them children, and then had been forced by the English victory either to return with their half-breed children to a country of strangers, full of prejudice against Indians, or to risk escaping under English guns to their husbands and adopted culture. For Bouquet had "reduced the Shawanese and Delawares etc. to the most Humiliating Terms of Peace," boasted Gen. Thomas Gage. "He has Obliged them to deliver up even their Own Children born of white women." But even the victorious soldier could understand the dilemma into which these women had been pushed. When Bouquet was informed that the English wife of an Indian chief had eloped in the night with her husband and children, he "requested that no pursuit should be made, as she was happier with her Chief than she would be if restored to her home."

Although most of the returned captives did not try to escape, the emotional torment caused by the separation from their adopted families deeply impressed the colonists. The Indians "delivered up their beloved captives with the utmost reluctance; shed torrents of tears over them, recommending them to the care and protection of the commanding officer." One young women "cryed and roared when asked to come and begged to Stay a little longer." "Some, who could not make their escape, clung to their savage acquaintance at parting, and continued many days in bitter lamentations, even refusing sustenance." Children "cried as if they should die when they were presented to us." With only small exaggeration an observer on the Muskingum could report that "every captive left the Indians with regret."

Another English problem was perhaps the most embarrassing in its manifestations, and certainly was so in its implications. For many Indians who had adopted white captives, the return of their "own Flesh, and Blood" to the English was unendurable. At the earliest opportunity, after bitter memories of the wars had faded on both sides, they journeyed through the English settlements to visit their estranged children, just as the Shawnee speaker had promised Bouquet they would. Jonathan Hoyt's Indian father visited him so often in Deerfield, sometimes bringing his captive sister, that Hoyt had to petition the Massachusetts General

Court for reimbursement for their support. In 1760 Sir William Johnson reported that a Canadian Indian "has been since down to Schenectady to visit one Newkirk of that place, who was some years a Prisoner in his House, and sent home about a year ago with this Indians' Sister, who came with her Brother now purely to see Said Newkirk whom she calls her Son and is verry fond of."

Obviously the feelings were mutual. Elizabeth Gilbert, adopted at the age of twelve, "always retained an affection toward John Huston, her Indian father (as she called him), for she remembered his kindness to her when in captivity." Even an adult who had spent less than six months with the Indians honored the chief who had adopted him. In 1799, eleven years after Thomas Ridout's release, his friend and father, Kakinathucca, "accompanied by three more Shawanese chiefs, came to pay me a visit at my house in York town (Toronto). He regarded myself and family with peculiar pleasure, and my wife and children contemplated with great satisfaction the noble and good qualities of this worthy Indian." The bond of affection that had grown in the Indian villages was clearly not an attachment that the English could dismiss as "unnatural."

Children who had been raised by Indian parents from infancy could be excused perhaps for their unwillingness to return, but the adults who displayed a similar reluctance, especially the women who had married Indian men and borne them children, drew another reaction. "For the honour of humanity," wrote William Smith, "we would suppose those persons to have been of the lowest rank, either bred up in ignorance and distressing penury, or who had lived so long with the Indians as to forget all their former connections. For, easy and unconstrained as the savage life is, certainly it could never be put in competition with the blessings of improved life and the light of religion, by any persons who have had the happiness of enjoying, and the capacity of discerning, them." If Smith was struck by the contrast between the visible impact of Indian education and his own cultural assumptions, he never said so.

To find a satisfactory explanation for the extraordinary drawing power of Indian culture, we should begin where the colonists themselves first came under its sway--on the trail to Indian country. For although the Indians were known for their patience, they wasted no time in beginning the educational process that would transform their hostile or fearful white captives into affectionate Indian relatives.

Perhaps the first transaction after the Indians had selected their prisoners and hurried them into cover was to replace their hard-heeled shoes with the footwear of the forest--moccasins. These were universally approved by the prisoners, who admitted that they traveled with "abundant more ease" than before. And on more than one occasion the knee-deep snows of northern New England forced the Indians to make snowshoes for their prisoners in order to maintain their pace of twenty-five to thirty miles a day. Such an introduction to the superbly adapted technology of the Indians alone would not convert the English, but it was a beginning.

The lack of substantial food supplies forced the captives to accommodate their stomachs as best they could to Indian trail fare, which ranged from nuts, berries, roots, and parched corn to beaver guts, horseflank, and semi-raw venison and moose, eaten without the customary English accompaniments of bread or salt. When there was nothing to eat, the Indians would "gird up their loins with a string," a technique that at least one captive found "very useful" when applied to himself. Although their food was often "unsavory" and in short supply, the Indians always shared it equally with the captives, who, being hungry, "relished (it) very well."

Another lesson was equally unexpected but instrumental in preparing the captives for even greater surprises when they reached the Indian settlements. It served to undermine the English horror of the Indians as bloodthirsty fiends who defile "any Woman they take alive" before "putting her to Death." Many redeemed prisoners made a point of insisting that, although they had been completely powerless in captivity, "the Indians are very civil towards their captive women, not offering any incivility by any indecent carriage." Thomas Ridout testified that "during the whole of the time I was with the Indians I never once witnessed an indecent or improper action amongst any of the Indians, whether young or old." Even William Smith admitted that "from every enquiry that has been made, it appears--that no woman thus saved is preserved from base motives, or need fear the violation of her honour." If there had been the least exception, we can be sure that this champion of civilization would have made the most of it.

One reason for the Indians' lack of sexual interest in their female captives was perhaps aesthetic, for the New England Indians, at least, esteemed black the color of beauty. A more fundamental reason derived from the main purpose of taking captives, which was to secure new members for their families and clans. Under the Indians' strong incest taboos, no warrior would attempt to violate his future sister or cousin. "Were he to indulge himself with a captive taken in war, and much more were he to offer violence in order to gratify his lust, he would incur indelible disgrace." Indeed, the taboo seems to have extended to the whole tribe. As George Croghan testified after long acquaintance with the Indians, "they have No (J)uri(s)diction or Laws butt that of Nature yett I have known more than onest thire Councils, order men to be putt to Death for Committing Rapes, (wh(ich) is a Crime they Despise." Since murder was a crime to be revenged by the victim's family in its own way and time, rape was the only capital offense punished by the tribe as a whole.

When the returning war parties approached the first Indian village, the educational process took on a new complexion. As one captive explained, "whenever the warriors return from an excursion against an enemy, their return to the tribe or village must be designated by war-like ceremonial; the captives or spoils, which may happen to crown their valor, must be conducted in a triumphant form, and decorated to every possible advantage." Accordingly, the cheek, chin, and forehead of every captive were painted with traditional dashes of vermillion mixed with bear's grease. Belts of wampum were hung around their necks, Indian clothes were substituted for English, and the men and boys had their hair plucked or shaved in Indian fashion. The physical transformation was so effective, said a twenty-six-year-old soldier. "that I began to think I was an Indian." Younger captives were less aware of the small distance between role-playing and real acceptance of the Indian life-style. When her captor dressed Frances Slocum, not yet five years old, in "beautiful wampum beads," she remembered at the end of a long and happy life as an Indian that he "made me look, as I thought, very fine. I was much pleased with the beautiful wampum."

The prisoners were then introduced to a "new school" of song and dance. "Little did we expect," remarked an English woman, "that the accomplishment of dancing would ever be taught us, by the savages. But the war dance must now be held; and every prisoner that could move must take its awkward steps. The figure consisted of circular motion around the fire; each sang his own music, and the best dancer was the one most violent in motion." To prepare for the event each captive had rehearsed a short Indian song on the trail. Mrs. Johnson recalled many years later that her song was "danna witchee natchepung' my son's was nar wiscumpton." Nehemiah How could not master the Indian pronunciation, so he was allowed to sing in English "I don't know where I go." In view of the Indians' strong sense of ceremonial propriety, it is small wonder that one captive thought that they "Seem(e)d to be Very much a mind I Should git it perfect."

Upon entering the village the Indians let forth with some distinctive music of their own. "When we came near the main Body of the Enemy," wrote Thomas Brown, a captive soldier from Fort William Henry, "the *Indians* made a Live-Shout, as they call it when they bring in a Prisoner alive (different from the Shout they make when they bring in Scalps, which they call a Dead-Shout)." According to another soldier, "their Voices are so sharp, shrill, loud and deep, that when they join together after one has made his Cry, it makes a most dreadful and horrible Noise, that stupifies the very Senses," a noise that naturally frightened many captives until they learned that it was not their death knell.

They had good reason to think that their end was near when the whole village turned out to form a gauntlet from the entrance to the center of the village and their captors ordered them to run through it. With ax handles, tomahawks, hoop poles, clubs, and switches the Indians flogged the racing captives as if to beat the whiteness out of them. In most villages, significantly, "it was only the more elderly People both Male and Female wh(ic)h rece(iv)ed this Useage--the young prisoners of Both Sexes Escaped without it" or were rescued from any serious harm by one or more villagers, perhaps indicating the Indian perception of the captives' various educability. When ten-year-old John Brickell was knocked down by the blows of his Seneca captors, "a very big Indian came up, and threw the company off me, and took me by the arm, and led me along through the lines with such rapidity that I scarcely touched the ground, and was not once struck after he took me."

The purpose of the gauntlet was the subject of some difference of opinion. A French soldier who had spent several years among the northeastern Indians believed that a prisoner "so unfortunate as to fall in the course of the bastonnade must get up quickly and keep on, or he will be beaten to death on the spot." On the other hand, Pierre de Charlevoix, the learned traveler and historian of Canada, wrote that "even when they seem to strike at random, and to be actuated only by fury, they take care never to touch any part where a blow might prove mortal." Both Frenchmen were primarily describing the Indians' treatment of other Indians and white men. Barbara Leininger and Marie LeRoy drew a somewhat different conclusion from their own treatment. Their welcome at the Indian village of Kittanning, they said, "consisted of three blows each, on the back. They were, however, administered with great mercy. Indeed, we concluded that we were beaten merely in order to keep up an ancient usage, and not with the intention of injuring us."

William Walton came closest to revealing the Indians' intentions in his account of the Gilbert family's captivity. The Indians usually beat the captives with "great Severity," he said, "by way of Revenge for their Relations who have been slain." Since the object of taking captives was to satisfy the Indian families who had lost relatives, the gauntlet served as the first of three initiation rites into Indian society, a purgative ceremony by which the bereaved Indians could exorcise their anguish and anger, and the captives could begin their cultural transformation.

If the first rite tried to beat the whiteness out of the captives, the second tried to wash it out. James Smith's experience was typical.

The old chief, holding me by the hand, made a long speech, very loud, and when he had done he handed me to three squaws, who led me by the hand down the bank into the river until the water was up to our middle. The squaws then made signs to me to plunge myself into the water, but I did not understand them. I thought that the result of the council was that I should be drowned, and that these young ladies were to be the executioners. They all laid violent hold of me, and I for some time opposed them with all my might, which occasioned loud laughter by the multitude that were on the bank of the river. At length one of the squaws made out to speak a little English (for I believe they began to be afraid of me) and said, 'No hurt you.' On this I gave myself up to their ladyships, who were as good as their word; for though they plunged me under water and washed and rubbed me severely, yet I could not say they hurt me much.

More than one captive had to receive similar assurance, but their worst fears were being laid to rest.

Symbolically purged of their whiteness by their Indian baptism, the initiates were dressed in new Indian clothes and decorated with feathers, jewelry, and paint. Then, with great solemnity, the village gathered around the council fire, where after a "profound silence" one of the chiefs spoke. Even a hostile captive, Zadock Steele, had to admit that although he could not understand the language spoken, he could "plainly discover a great share of native eloquence." The chief's speech, he said, was "of considerable length, and its effect obviously manifested weight of argument, solemnity of thought, and at least human sensibility." But even this the twenty-two-year-old New Englander could not appreciate on its own terms, for in the next breath he denigrated the ceremony as "an assemblage of barbarism, assuming the appearance of civilization."

A more charitable account was given by James Smith, who through an interpreter was addressed in the following words:

My son, you are now flesh of our flesh and bone of our bone. By the ceremony that was performed this day, every drop of white blood was washed out of your veins. You are taken into the Caughnewaga nation and initiated into a war-like tribe. You are adopted into a great family and now received with great seriousness and solemnity in the room and place of a great man. After what has passed this day you are now one of us by an old strong law and custom. My son, you have now nothing to fear. We are now under the same obligations to love, support and defend you that we are to love and defend one another. Therefore you are to consider yourself as one of our people.

"At this time," admitted the eighteen-year-old Smith, "I did not believe this fine speech, especially that of the white blood being washed out of me; but since that time I have found that there was so much sincerity in said speech; for from that day I never knew them to make any distinction between me and themselves in any respect whatever until I left them...we all shared one fate." It is a chord that sounds through nearly every captivity narrative: "They treated me...in every way as one of themselves."

When the adoption ceremony had ended, the captive was taken to the wigwam of his new family, who greeted him with a "most dismal howling, crying bitterly, and wringing their hands in all the agonies of grief for a deceased relative." "The higher in favour the adopted Prisoners (were) to be placed, the greater Lamentation (was) made over them." After a threnodic memorial to the lost member, which may have "added to the Terror of the Captives," who "imagined it to be no other than a Prelude to inevitable Destruction," the mood suddenly shifted. "I never saw...such hug(g)ing and kissing from the women and crying for joy," exclaimed one young recipient. Then an interpreter introduced each member of the new family--in one case "from brother to seventh cousins"--and "they came to me one after another," said another captive, "and shook me by the hand, in token that they considered me to stand in the same relationship to them as the one in whose stead I was placed."

Most young captives assumed the places of Indian sons and daughters, but occasionally the match was not exact. Mary Jemison replaced a brother who had been killed in "Washington's war," while twenty-six-year-old Titus King assumed the unlikely role of a grandfather. Although their sex and age may not always have corresponded, the adopted captives succeeded to all the deceased's rights and obligations-- the same dignities, honors, and often the same names. "But the one adopted," reported a French soldier, "must be prudent and wise in his conduct, if he wants to make himself as well liked as the man he is replacing. This seldom fails to occur, because he is continually reminded of the dead man's conduct and good deeds."

So literal could the replacement become at times that no amount of exemplary conduct could alter the captive's reception. Thomas Peart, a twenty-three-year-old Pennsylvanian, was adopted as an uncle in an Iroquois family, but "the old Man, whose Place (he) was to fill, had never been considered by his

Family as possessed of any Merit." Accordingly, Peart's dress, although in the Indian style, was "in a meaner Manner, as they did not hold him in high Esteem after his Adoption." Since his heart was not in becoming an Indian anyway, and "observing that they treated him just as they had done the old worthless Indian...he therefore concluded he would only fill his Predecessor's Station, and used no Endeavours to please them."

When the prisoners had been introduced to all their new relatives and neighbors, the Indians proceeded to shower them with gifts. Luke Swetland, taken from Pennsylvania during the Revolution, was unusually feted with "three hats, five blankets, near twenty pipes, six razors, six knives, several spoons, gun and ammunition, fireworks, several Indian pockets (pouches), one Indian razor, awls, needles, goose quills, paper and many other things of small value"--enough to make him the complete Indian warrior. Most captives, however, settled for a new shirt or dress, a pair of decorated moccasins, and abundant promises of future kindness, which later prompted the captives to acknowledge once again that the Indians were "a(s) good as their word." "All the family was kind to me," related Thomas Gist, "as if I had realy been the nearest of relation they had in the world." The two women who adopted Mary Jemison were no less loving. "I was ever considered by them as a real sister," she said near the end of a long life with them, "the same as though I had been born of their mother."

Treatment such as this--and it was almost universal--left an indelible mark on every captive, whether or not they eventually returned to English society. Although captives like Mrs. Johnson found their adoption an "unnatural situation," they had to defend the humanity of the practice. "Those who have profited by refinement and education," she argued, "ought to abate part of the prejudice, which prompts them to look with an eye of censure on this untutored race . . . Do they ever adopt an enemy," she asked, "and salute him by the tender name of brother?" It is not difficult to imagine what effect such feelings must have had in younger people less habituated to English culture, especially those who had lost their own parents.

The formalities, purgations, and initiations were now completed. Only one thing remained for the Indians: by their daily example and instruction to "make an Indian of you," as the Delawares told John Brickell. This required a steady union of two things: the willingness and gratitude of the captives, and the consistent love and trust of the Indians. By the extraordinary ceremonies through which they had passed, most captives had had their worst fears allayed. From a state of apprehension or even terror they had suddenly emerged with their persons intact and a solemn invitation to begin a new life, as full of love, challenge, and satisfaction as any they had known. For "when they (the Indians) once determine to give life, they give everything with it, which, in their apprehension, belongs to it." The sudden release from anxiety into a realm of affirmative possibility must have disposed many captives to accept the Indian way of life.

According to the adopted colonists who recounted the stories of their new lives, Indian life was more than capable of claiming their respect and allegiance even if they eventually returned to English society. The first indication that the Indians were serious in their professions of equality came when the adopted captives were given freedom of movement within and without the Indian villages. Naturally the degree of freedom and its timing depended on the captive's willingness to enter into the spirit of Indian life.

Despite his adult years, Thomas Ridout had earned his captor's trust by the third night of their march to the Shawnee villages. Having tied his prisoner with a rope to himself the first two nights, the Indian "never afterwards used this precaution, leaving me at perfect liberty, and frequently during the nights that were frosty and cold," Ridout recalled, "I found his hand over me to examine whether or not I was covered." As soon as seventeen-year-old John Leeth, an Indian trader's clerk, reached his new family's village, "my father gave me and his two (Indian) sons our freedom, with a rifle, two pounds of powder, four pounds of lead, a blanket, shirt, match-coat, pair of leggings, etc. to each, as our freedom dues; and told us to shift for ourselves." Eleven-year-old Benjamin Gilbert, "considered as the (Indian) King's Successor," was of course "entirely freed from Restraint, so that he even began to be delighted with his Manner of Life." Even Zadock Steele, a somewhat reluctant Indian at twenty-two, was "allowed the privilege of visiting any part of the village, in the day time, and was received with marks of fraternal affection, and treated with all the civility an Indian is capable to bestow."

Captives who were strangers were permitted not only to visit frequently but occasionally to live together. When Thomas Gist suddenly moved from his adoptive aunt's house back to her brother's, she "imajined I was affronted," he wrote, and "came and asked me the reason why I had left her, or what injury she or any of the family had done me that I should leave her without so much as leting her know of it. I told her it was the company of my fellow prisoners that drew me to the town. She said that it was not so far but I mite have walked to see them every two or three days, and ask some of them to come and see me those days that I did not chuse to go abroad, and that all such persons as I thought proper to bring to the house should be as welcom(e) as one of the family, and made many promises how she would be if I return. However," boasted the twenty-four-year-old Gist, "I was obstinate and would not." It is not surprising that captives who enjoyed such autonomy were also trusted under the same roof. John Brickell remarked that three white prisoners, "Patton, Johnston, and Mrs. Baker (of Kentucky) had all lived with me in the same house among the Indians, and we were as intimate as brothers and sisters."

Once the captives had earned the basic trust of their Indian families, nothing in Indian life was denied them. When they reached the appropriate age, the Indians offered to find them suitable marriage partners. Understandably, some of the older captives balked at this, sensing that it was calculated to bind them with marital ties to a culture they were otherwise hesitant to accept. When Joseph Gilbert, a forty-one-year-old father and husband, was adopted into a leading family, his new relatives informed him that "if he would marry amongst them, he should enjoy the Privileges which they enjoyed; but this Proposal he was not disposed to comply with, . . . as he was not over anxious to conceal his Dislike to them." Elizabeth Peart, his twenty-year-old married sister, was equally reluctant. During her adoption ceremony "they obliged her to sit down with a young Man an Indian, and the eldest Chieftain of the Family repeating a Jargon of Words to her unintelligible, but which she considered as some form amongst them of Marriage," she was visited with "the most violent agitations, as she was determined, at all events, to oppose any step of this Nature." Marie LeRoy's honor was even more dearly bought. When "it was at length determined by the (Indians) that (she) should marry one of the Natives, who had been selected for her," she told a fellow captive that "she would sooner be shot than have him for her husband." Whether her revulsion was directed toward the act itself or toward the particular suitor was not said.

The distinction is pertinent because the weight of evidence suggests that marriage was not compulsory for the captives, and common sense tells us that any form of compulsion would have defeated the Indians' purpose in trying to persuade the captives to adopt their way of life. Mary Jemison, at the time a captive for two years, was unusual in implying that she was forced to marry an Indian. "Not long after the Delawares came to live with us, at Wiishto," she recalled, "my sisters told me that I must go and live with one of them, whose name is She-nin-jee. Not daring to cross them, or disobey their commands, with a great degree of reluctance I went; and Sheninjee and I were married according to Indian custom." Considering the tenderness and kindness with which most captives reported they were treated, it is likely that she was less compelled in reality than in her perception and memory of it.

For even hostile witnesses could not bring themselves to charge that force was ever used to promote marriages. The Puritan minister John Williams said only that "great *essays* (were) made to get (captives) married" among the Canadian Indians by whom he was captured. Elizabeth Hanson and her husband "could by no means obtain from their hands" their sixteen-year-old daughter, "for the squaw, to whom she was given, had a son whom she intended my daughter should in time *be prevailed with to marry.*" Mrs. Hanson was probably less concerned that her daughter would be forced to marry an Indian than that she might "in time" want to, for as she acknowledged from her personal experience, "the Indians are very civil towards their captive women, not offering any incivility by any indecent carriage." An observer of the return of the white prisoners to Bouquet spoke for his contemporaries when he reported--with an almost audible sigh of relief--that "there had not been a solitary instance among them of any woman having her delicacy injured by being compelled to marry. They had been left liberty of choice, and those who chose to remain single were not sufferers on that account."

So free from compulsion were the captives that several married fellow white prisoners. In 1715 the priest of the Jesuit mission at Sault-au-Recollet "married Ignace shoetak8anni (Joseph Rising, aged twenty-one) and Elizabeth T8atog8ach (Abigail Nims, aged fifteen), both English, who wish to remain with the Christian Indians, not only renouncing their nation, but even wishing to live *en sauvages."* (The "8" used by the French in Indian words signifies "w," which did not exist in French). But from the Indians' standpoint, and perhaps from their own, captives such as John Leeth and Thomas Armstrong may have had the best of all possible marriages. After some years with the Indians, Leeth "was married to a young woman, seventeen or eighteen years of age; also a prisoner to the Indians; who had been taken by them when about twenty months old." Armstrong, an adopted Seneca, also married a "full blooded white woman, who like himself had been a captive among the Indians from infancy, but who unlike him, had not acquired a knowledge of one word of the English language, being essentially an Indian in all save blood." Their commitment to each other deepened their commitment to the Indian culture of which they had become equal members.

The captives' social equality was also demonstrated by their being asked to share in the affairs of war and peace, matters of supreme importance to Indian society. When the Senecas who had adopted Thomas Peart decided to "make a War Excursion," they asked him to go with them. But since he was in no mood--and no physical condition--to play the Indian, "he determinately refused them, and was therefore left at Home with the Family." The young Englishman who became Old White Chief was far more eager to defend his new culture, but his origins somewhat limited his military activity. "When I grew to manhood," he recalled, "I went with them (his Iroquois kinsmen) on the warpath against the neighboring tribes, but never against the white settlers, lest by some unlucky accident I might be recognized and claimed by former friends." Other captives--many of them famous renegades--were less cautious. Charlevoix noticed in his travels in Canada that adopted captives "frequently enter into the spirit of the nation, of which they are become members, in such a manner, that they make no difficulty of going to war against their own countrymen." It was behavior such as this that prompted Sir William Johnson to praise Bouquet after his expedition to the Ohio for compelling the Indians to give up every white person, even the "Children born of White Women. That mixed Race," he wrote, referring to first-generation captives as well, "forgetting their Ancestry on one side are found to be the most Inveterate of any, and would greatly Augment their numbers."

The Indians of the Northeast readily admitted white captives to their highest councils and offices. Just after Thomas Ridout was captured on the Ohio, he was surprised to meet an English-speaking "white man, about twenty-two years of age, who had been taken prisoner when a lad and had been adopted, and now was a chief among Shawanese." He need not have been surprised, for there were many more like him. John Tarbell was not only "one of the wealthiest" of the Caughnawagas but "the eldest chief and speaker of the tribe." Timothy Rice, formerly of Westborough, Massachusetts, was also made one of the clan chiefs at Caughnawaga, partly by inheritance from his Indian father but largely for "his own Super(io)r Talents" and "war-like Spirit for which he was much celebrated." In public office as in every sphere of Indian life, the English captives found that the color of their skin was unimportant; only their talent and their inclination of heart mattered.

Understandably, neither their skill nor their loyalty was left to chance. From the moment the captives, especially the young ones, came under their charge, the Indians made a concerted effort to inculcate in them Indian habits of mind and body. If the captives could be taught to think, act, and react like Indians, they would effectively cease to be English and would assume an Indian identity. This was the Indians' goal, toward which they bent every effort in the weeks and months that followed their formal adoption of the white captives.

The educational character of Indian society was recognized by even the most inveterately English captives. Titus King, a twenty-six-year-old New England soldier, spent a year with the Canadian Indians at St. Francis trying--unsuccessfully--to undo their education of "Eight or ten young (English) Children." What "an awfull School this (is) for Children," he wrote. "When We

See how Quick they will fall in with the Indian ways, nothing Seems to be more takeing in Six months time they Forsake Father and mother Forgit there own Land Refuess to Speak there own toungue and Seemin(g)ly be Holley Swollowed up with the Indians." The older the person, of course, the longer it took to become fully Indianized. Mary Jemison, captured at the age of fifteen, took three or four years to forget her natural parents and the home she had once loved. "If I had been taken in infancy," she said, "I should have been contented in my situation." Some captives, commonly those over fifteen or sixteen years old, never made the transition from English to Indian. Twenty-four-year-old Thomas Gist, soldier and son of a famous scout and Indian agent, accommodated himself to his adoption and Indian life for just one year and then made plans to escape. "All curiosity with regard to acting the part of an Indian," he related, "which I could do very well, being th(o)rougherly satisfied, I was determined to be what I really was."

Children, however, took little time to "fall in with the Indian ways." Titus King mentioned six months. The Reverend John Williams witnessed the effects of eight or nine months when he stopped at St.Francis in February 1704. There, he said, "we found several poor children, who had been taken from the eastward (Maine) the summer before; a sight very affecting, they being in habit very much like Indians, and in manners very much symbolizing with them." When young Joseph Noble visited his captive sister in Montreal, "he still belonged to the St. Francis tribe of Indians, and was dressed remarkably fine, having forty or fifty broaches in his shirt, clasps on his arm, and great variety of knots and bells about his clothing. He brought his little sister . . . a young fawn, a basket of cranberries, and a lump of sap sugar." Sometime later he was purchased from the Indians by a French gentleman who promptly "dressed him in the French style; but he never appeared so bold and majestic, so spirited and vivacious, as when arrayed in his Indian habit and associating with his Indian friends."

The key to any culture is its language, and the young captives were quick to learn the Indian dialects of their new families. Their retentive memories and flair for imitation made them ready students, while the Indian languages, at once oral, concrete, and mythopoeic, lightened the task. In less than six months ten-year-old Oliver Spencer had "acquired a sufficient knowledge of the Shawnee tongue to understand all ordinary conversation and, indeed, the greater part of all that I heard (accompanied, as their conversation and speeches were, with the most significant gestures)," which enabled him to listen "with much pleasure and sometimes with deep interest" to his Indian mother tell of battles, heroes, and history in the long winter evenings. When Jemina Howe was allowed to visit her four-year-old son at a neighboring Indian village in Canada, he greeted her "in the Indian tongue" with "Mother, are you come?" He too had been a captive for only six months.

As in any school, language was only one of many subjects of instruction. Since the Indians generally assumed that whites were physically inferior to themselves, captive boys were often prepared for the hardy life of hunters and warriors by a rigorous program of physical training. John McCullough, aged eight, was put through the traditional Indian course by his adoptive uncle. "In the beginning of winter," McCullough recalled, "he used to raise me by day light every morning, and make me sit down in the creek up to my chin in the cold water, in order to make me hardy as he said, whilst he would sit on the bank smoking his pipe until he thought I had been long enough in the water, he would then bid me to dive. After I came out of the water he would order me not to go near the fire until I would be dry. I was kept at that till the water was frozen over, he would then break the ice for me and send me in as before." As shocking, as it may have been to his system, such treatment did nothing to turn him against Indian life. Indeed, he was transparently proud that he had borne up under the strenuous regimen "with the firmness of an Indian." Becoming an Indian was as much a challenge and an adventure for the young colonists as it was a "sore trial," and many of them responded to it with alacrity and zest. Of children their age we should not expect any less.

The captives were taught not only to speak and to endure as Indians but to act as Indians in the daily social and economic life of the community. Naturally, boys were taught the part of men and girls the part of women, and according to most colonial sources--written, it should be noted, predominantly by men--the boys enjoyed the better fate. An Ohio pioneer remembered that the prisoners from his party were "put into different families, the women to hard drudging and the boys to run wild with the young Indians, to amuse themselves with bow and arrow, dabble in the water, or obey any other notion their wild natures might dictate." William Walton, the author of the Gilbert family captivity narrative, also felt that the "Labour and Drudgery" in an Indian family fell to "the Share of the Women." He described fourteen-year-old Abner Gilbert as living a "dronish Indian life, idle and poor, having no other Employ than the gathering of Hickory-Nuts; and although young," Walton insisted, "his Situation was very irksome." Just how irksome the boy found his freedom from colonial farm chores was revealed when the ingenuous Walton related that "Abner, having no useful Employ, amused himself with catching fish in the lake. . . Not being of an impatient Disposition," said Walton soberly, "he bore his Captivity without repining."

While most captive boys had "nothing to do, but cut a little wood for the fire," draw water for cooking and drinking, and "shoot Blackbirds that came to eat up the corn," they enjoyed "some leisure" for "hunting and other innocent devertions in the woods." Women and girls, on the other hand, shared the burdens--onerous ones in English eyes--of their Indian counterparts. But Mary Jemison, who had been taught English ways for fifteen years before becoming an Indian, felt that the Indian women's labor "was not severe," their tasks "probably not harder than that (sic) of white women," and their cares "certainly. . . not half as numerous, nor as great." The work of one year was "exactly similar, in almost every respect, to that of the others, without that endless variety that is to be observed in the common labor of the white people. . . In the summer, we planted, tended and harvested our corn, and generally had all our children with us; but had no master to oversee or drive us, so that we could work as leisurely as we pleased. . . In the season of hunting, it was our business, in addition to our cooking, to bring home the game that was taken by the (men), dress it, and carefully preserve the eatable meat, and prepare or dress the skins." "Spinning, weaving, sewing, stocking knitting," and like domestic tasks of colonial women were generally unknown. Unless Jemison was correct, it would be virtually impossible to understand why so many women and girls chose to become Indians. A life of unremitting drudgery, as the English saw it, could certainly hold no attraction for civilized women fresh from frontier farms and villages.

The final and most difficult step in the captives' transition from English to Indian was to acquire the ability to think as Indians, to share unconsciously the values, beliefs, and standards of Indian culture. From an English perspective, this should have been nearly an impossible task for civilized people because they perceived Indian culture as immoral and irreligious and totally antithetical to the civilized life they had known, however briefly. "Certainly," William Smith assumed, "it could never be put in competition with the blessings of improved life and the light of religion." But many captives soon discovered that the English had no monopoly on virtue and that in many ways the Indians were morally superior to the English, more more Christian than the Christians.

As early as 1643 Roger Williams had written a book to suggest such a thing, but he could be dismissed as a misguided visionary who let the Narragansetts go to his head. It was more difficult to dismiss someone like John Brickell, who had lived with the Indians for four and one-half years and had no ax to grind with established religion. "The Delawares are the best people to train up children I ever was with," he wrote. "Their leisure hours are, in a great measure, spent in training up their children to observe what they believe to be right . . . (A)s a nation they may be considered fit examples for many of us Christians to follow. They certainly follow what they are taught to believe right more closely, and I might say more honestly, in general, than we Christians do the divine precepts of our Redeemer . . . I know I am influenced to good, even at this day," he concluded, "more from what I learned among them, than what I learned among people of my own color." After many decades with them, Mary Jemison insisted that "the moral character of the Indians was . . . uncontaminated. Their fidelity was perfect, and became proverbial; they were strictly honest; they despised deception and falsehood; and chastity was held in high veneration." Even the tory historian Peter Oliver, who was no friend to the Indians, admitted that "they have a Religion of their own, which, to the eternal Disgrace of many Nations who boast of Politeness, is more influential on their Conduct than that of those who hold them in so great Contempt." To the acute discomfort of the colonists, more than one captive maintained that the Indians were a "far more moral race than the whites."

In the principled school of Indian life the captives experienced a decisive shift in their cultural and personal identities. Although fear undoubtedly accounted for some of the converts' initial behavior, desire to win the approval of new relatives also played a part. "I had lived in my new habitation about a week," recalled Oliver Spencer, "and having given up all hope of escaping . . . began to regard it as my future home . . . I strove to be cheerful, and by my ready obedience to ingratiate myself with Cooh-coo-cheeh (his Indian mistress), for whose kindness I felt grateful." A year after James Smith had been adopted, a number of prisoners were brought in by his new kinsmen and a gauntlet formed to welcome them. Smith "went and told them how they were to act" and then "fell into one of the ranks with the Indians, shouting and yelling like them." One middle-aged man's turn came, and "as they were not very severe on him," confessed the new Indian, "as he passed me I hit him with a piece of pumpkin--which pleased the Indians much." If their zeal to emulate the Indians sometimes exceeded their mercy, the captives had nonetheless fulfilled their new families' expectations: they had begun to act as Indians in spirit as well as body. Only time would be necessary to transform their conscious efforts into unconscious habits and complete their cultural conversion.

"By what power does it come to pass," asked Crevecoeur, "that children who have been adopted when young among these people, . . . and even grown persons . . . can never be prevailed on to re-adopt European manners?" Given the malleability of youth, we should not be surprised that children underwent a rather sudden and permanent transition from English to Indian--although we might be pressed to explain why so few Indian children made the transition in the opposite direction. But the adult colonists who became Indians cannot be explained as easily, for the simple reason that they, unlike many of the children, were fully conscious of their cultural identities while they were being subjected to the Indians' assiduous attempts to convert them. Consequently, their cultural metamorphosis involved a large degree of personal choice.

The great majority of white Indians left no explanations for their choice. Forgetting their original language and their past, they simply disappeared into their adopted society. But those captives who returned to write narratives of their experiences left several clues to the motives of those who chose to stay behind. They stayed because they found Indian life to possess a strong sense of community, abundant love, and uncommon integrity--values that the English colonists also honored, if less successfully. But Indian life was attractive for other values--for social equality, mobility, adventure, and, as two adult converts acknowledged, "the most perfect freedom, the ease of living, (and) the absence of those cares and corroding solicitudes which so often prevail with us."

By contrast, as Crevecoeur said, there must have been in the Indians' "social bond something singularly captivating." Whatever it was, its power had no better measure than the large number of English colonists who became, contrary to the civilized assumptions of their countrymen, white Indians.

*I wish to thank Wilcomb Washburn for his suggestions and the American Council of Learned Societies for its support. A longer, fully annotated version of this article was published in the *William and Mary Quarterly,* Third Series, 32 (January 1975): 55-88. Footnotes have been omitted in the present version.

3

BONDS BETWEEN INDIANS AND OTHER RACIAL GROUPS IN AN URBAN SETTING

By

C. Hoy Steele

INTRODUCTION

In a society that oppressed racial minorities, it is not surprising that interracial contact--when not avoided altogether--is most often strained. Relations between Indians and other racial groups in Prairie City (pseudonym), Kansas, exhibit the expected pattern.[1]

In rare cases, however, positive bonds form. These exceptions are of disproportionate interest to their frequency. Together with an analysis of the dynamics of the Indian community of the city they provide clues for those interested in improving relations between Indians and non-Indians. Their description may also be particularly instructive for non-Indians who wish to relate to Indians in a non-exploitive way. Finally, they may be relevant to the wider goal of improved race relations generally.

The population of Prairie City is about 125,000 people, according to the 1970 census. Of this aggregate, 10,500 are black; Chicanos are estimated (the census counted them in the white category) to number approximately 8,500. Indians are the third largest minority group, but total only about 1,000 people, or less than one percent of the city's residents.

Approximately half the Indians in Prairie City are Pottawatomi, claiming as "home" the Prairie Band Pottawatomi reservation a half hour's drive away. Another one-fourth belongs to a related tribe, the Kickapoo, whose reservation is also less than fifty miles from the city. The remaining 250 or so Indian residents have arrived from Oklahoma, Nebraska, the Dakotas, and other western states since World War II, and are members of a wide variety of tribal groups.

By objective and subjective measures, the Indians are the most impoverished ethnic group in Prairie City. Less than half the household heads of Indian families are employed full-time, despite the fact that the Indians probably have a lower percentage of single parent families than poor whites, blacks, and Chicanos. Few Indian students graduate from high school, and Indian children are subject to greater health problems than any other group. Indians are arrested at over seven times the rate of the population as a whole, and over three times the rate of blacks.

The research on which this report is based was conducted over an 18-month period in 1970 and 1971. I engaged in participant observation, supplemented by informal interviews, and observed contact between Indians and non-Indians in a variety of settings. A fuller description of the research project and a much lengthier report of the findings are contained in my works cited at the end of this article. Having continued my physical contact with the Indian community of Prairie City until mid-1974, I believe that the basic dynamics reported here hold for the mid- and late seventies.

UNSATISFACTORY RELATIONS BETWEEN INDIANS AND OTHER GROUPS

On an individual level, Indians in Prairie City are highly mistrustful of most whites and other ethnic groups. When Indians occupy client roles (e.g., with the welfare department and other social service agencies) or when they seek medical care, serious problems of communication usually arise. Similar difficulties abound between Indian tenants and non-Indian landlords, and between Indian workers and job-seekers and their employers or prospective employers, respectively. Contacts between Indians and other minority groups are competitive, frequently hostile, and rarely mutually beneficial.

Researchers (usually white) have a bad image among the Indians of Prairie City; they are viewed with disdain and mistrust. One Kickapoo man said to me:"The anthropologist, he comes around asking questions and the Indian says, 'Uh huh.' He asks more questions and the Indian just says, 'Uh huh.' (Scornfully).

Then he goes and thinks he knows all about Indians!"

Another difficult role is enacted by self-advertised "friends" of Indians. I encountered several non-Indians during my field work who fancied themselves in this manner; the Indians who were the recipients of such "friendship," however, seemed to have a different view of the relationship. One middle-aged white man who visited a meeting of the Prairie City Indian Center seemed eager to "help out," and offered strong opinions on several issues. He was given a respectful hearing, but it was clear that none of the Indians agreed with him. I never saw him again.

A common setting for casual and brief interaction between Indians and non-Indians occurs when Indians publicly display their identity--for example, at art and craft exhibits or at Pow Wows. I was amazed at how many times I heard whites initiate conversation with Indians by proudly claiming 1/8 or 1/16 or 1/32 Indian heritage (usually Cherokee). This declaration seemed to be offered as a way to "break the ice," but usually failed to produce the warm response that was expected. When further attempts at ingratiation also failed, the non-Indian would usually appear nervous or confused, and move on.

On the other hand, many whites in Prairie City are surprised to know that Indians live there at all. The Indians experience this lack of awareness in a way reminiscent of Ralph Ellison's *The Invisible Man*. They feel invisible--or worse, selectively invisible. One Indian man put it this way.

> You can be walking down the street and see an Indian dressed in a suit and never see him, he's not there. He's an invisible man . . . But right behind him comes one that's all wined up, and that's staggering and makes a heck of a spectacle and they stereotype him--there's the Indian.

Both Indians and non-Indians experience confusion, frustration, and anger when Indians seek services from non-Indian agencies or individuals. Many Indians who are eligible for welfare never even apply, sometimes suffering health impairment as a consequence. When Indians do seek assistance, the problems of bureaucratic inefficiency and unsympathetic welfare employees are sometimes overwhelming, and many Indians fail to receive critical services.

Although discrimination by whites against Indians seems less pervasive than that against blacks, it is nevertheless widespread and often blatant in Prairie City. Housing discrimination, especially prevalent, is sometimes justified by landlords who complain of overcrowding. A landlady (in this case, a black) said, "Well, you get two in there and pretty soon all the relatives come and before long you've got fifteen and things get beat up and the place is a mess."

The Indian-black relationship is both complex and uncomfortable. From the Indians' point of view, blacks generally ignore or ride roughshod over them, as seen particularly in the former OEO (Office of Economic Opportunity) Community Action program. Neither Indians nor Chicanos participated significantly in the program due to its overwhelming domination by blacks. Indians sometimes view blacks as trying to co-opt them into black struggles. In the spring of 1970, blacks attempted to force the closing of public schools in the city, and issued a statement claiming the support of the Indian community.

This act provoked an intensive negative reaction among the Indians, and a statement repudiating the claim was promptly issued to the press by two Indian men. Many Indians in Prairie City hold attitudes toward blacks that seem to parallel typical white stereotypes and opinions. Like whites, Indians exhibit prejudice against blacks--as revealed in numerous comments and jokes, and in language. Prejudice is also seen in the fact that Indian-black marriages meet with stronger disapproval than any other combination. The children of Indian-black marriages also experience greater difficulty finding acceptance as Indians than do the children of Indian-white or Indian-Chicano unions. This is particularly the case if, visually, they appear more black than Indian.

Indians seem to feel more kindly toward Chicanos than toward blacks. Most Indians seem to approve of the recent tendency of Chicanos to celebrate and emphasize the Indian part of their heritage. Then too, Chicanos are also in a minority position with respect to blacks as well as whites, and their general style more closely resembles that of Indians than that of blacks (particularly in their relative lack of aggression). At the same time, Indians can identify with the fact that Chicanos have experienced oppression from the larger society, just as Indians have.

Even with respect to Chicanos, however, the Indians exert unrelenting independence. Indians insist on their own uniqueness and refuse to compromise that awareness or soften its emphasis in the interest of short-term goals or the avoidance of short-term problems. A "minority coalition" in Prairie City, spearheaded by blacks, heretofore has been unsuccessful in attracting Indian participation. Indians seem to feel that other groups would benefit more than Indians, and that a coalition would divert attention from the real--and unique--needs of the Indian community.

Many Indians even resent being categorized with other groups under the label of "minority." They are Indians as well as members of a tribe and, perhaps, a band; many would emphasize the primacy of the tribal over the racial designation. They are highly indignant when confused with other groups, when others speak for them, and when others imitate them or make false pretentions of Indianness.

INDIAN CULTURE AND COMMUNITY

Knowledge of certain characteristic values of Indian culture helps an outsider understand how his or her behavior may be judged. Without exploring Indian cultures in depth, we can briefly look at a few of the important cultural proscriptions which occur in a wide range of tribal groups.

An Indian may not appear to covet praise or publicity and still hope to keep the respect of others. A leader is not someone who wrests power for himself but a person who has it thrust upon him by his fellows. Pretension is the surest guarantee of criticism. I was cautioned to "be myself" when with Indians, and never to attempt to impress anyone. Frequently I observed non-Indians in various settings trying to make a "good impression" on Indians or act very knowledgeable. They invariably "turned off" the Indians.

An important related value is the ethic of non-interference. This characteristic was apparent at the first Indian Center meeting that I attended. No matter how banal or long-winded the monologues (including those of several white guests who were ill-attuned to Indian etiquette), everyone who wanted to speak had his or her say, and was not interrupted. Non-interference carries over into many facets of life, including childraising and relations among adults. Children are not "channeled" or pushed into "becoming" something in fulfillment of a parent's wishes. Unsolicited advice to others is not welcomed.

Many categories of non-Indians unwittingly breach this norm of non-interference--e.g., teachers, social workers, employers, physicians, and activists belonging to other minority groups. According to one Indian man, if a boss says, "Can I show you how?" he responds, "Sure, and while you're at it you can finish the job yourself." In the eyes of this rather typically outspoken individual, an Indian will do a poorer job if he is not allowed to do it his own way. Generally, interfering non-Indians may expect to receive very little clear feedback if they have violated Indian propriety--since well-mannered Indians seldom interfere by criticizing. I witnessed many interchanges between Indians and non-Indians in which the latter received a polite but cool reception and, when they left, were unaware that they had offended the Indians with their interfering or patronizing behavior.

In addition to the unique cultural characteristics described, brief mention should be made of the internal dynamics of the Indian community. Nearly all primary relations are carried on within it. Social groups, such as Pow Wow clubs, athletic teams, and several religious groups are membered entirely by Indians. The principal service organization is the Indian Center, which exists to improve the quality of urban life of Indian residents. Most Pottawatomis and Kickapoos have relatives living on their respective reservations and maintain some level of activity in reservation affairs. Going beyond the immediate Prairie City-reservation Indian milieu usually means joining in an event involving Indians from nearby cities and states-- participating in a Pow Wow or dinner dance, competing in an Indian bowling, basketball, or softball tournament or, for community leaders, attending a regional meeting to discuss or take action on the unique problems of Indians in modern society.

Finally, it should be emphasized that it is this participation in the life of the Indian community that, more than anything else--more than fullblood heritage or even "cultural purity"--identifies someone as an Indian. No matter how authoritative or respected he or she may otherwise be, an Indian who does not "mingle with the Indians" has very low status within the Indian community. (Thus it is that non-Indians may receive a very limited view of Indians from those who would rather be something else, or who would rather spend their time with non-Indians). Likewise, an Indian who lacks some of the other credentials of Indianness may be accorded rather widespread acceptance if he is an active participant in Indian communal life. Participation with others signifies public affirmation of pride in one's Indianness and identification with one's race.

In sum, the separation of the Indian population from the other residents of Prairie City stems from three sources. In the first place, the Indians are culturally unique. Indian culture has changed over the decades and centuries--so has white culture--but it remains Indian culture. This statement holds for Indians generally, and the Indians of Prairie City are no exception.

Second, Indians have been and continue to be oppressed by American society. Today, as in the past, they respond to attacks upon themselves by fortifying the barriers between themselves and non-Indians.

It is but a short step to the third factor promoting separation, the norm of participating within the life of the Indian community. Informal positive and negative sanctions reinforce this norm, which is accepted by the majority of Indians in Prairie City.

BONDING BETWEEN INDIANS AND OTHER GROUPS

Although most non-Indian researchers and "helpers" are not accorded a welcome in the Indian community, some gain a measure of acceptance that allows them to function effectively. Two examples, though far from exhaustive, may serve to illustrate how these kinds of relationships can be established. Larry, a dedicated and deeply religious white man, exemplifies the helper role. He subsisted on about $60 a month supplied by the largest Roman Catholic church in Prairie City, and spent most of his time working at the Indian Center. My own experiences provide the second example. In addition to being a researcher, I assumed a helper role part of the time as well, by working as a volunteer at the Indian Center. I attended all the important Center functions and was "on duty" there one day a week.

One factor that led to the acceptance that Larry and I both experienced was the totality of our involvement and the fact that our interest in the Indian community and in Indian people was personal as well as functional. Larry was as poor as many of the poorest Indians, and was clearly uninterested in personal gain. He occupied a shabby room two blocks from the Indian Center in an area of relatively heavy Indian residence. While his ascetic lifestyle kept him from socializing with Indians at bars, bowling alleys, and parties, he related to Indian people in a friendly and personal way that won the trust of most with whom he came in contact.

My case was different. As a researcher, I was there to get something for myself. Mindful, however, of anthropologist Rosalie Wax's advice that people need to get something in return from a fieldworker, I occupied a helper role as well as a researcher role. While this satisfied the need for reciprocity it would not have been enough by itself. I believe the most crucial condition for my acceptance--which was never complete-- was that I was perceived as friendly and interested in Indian people for themselves, beyond whatever usefulness they might be to my educational career. One night at a party I was told by the president of the Indian Center that while she and all Indians mistrust whites, she felt differently about me because "you came and showed you wanted to live with the Indians and not just study them." She felt that I had a real interest in Indian *people* and did not merely "want to know what they do from the time they wake up to the time they go to sleep at night."

A second factor that facilitated acceptance for Larry and me was a depth of understanding that included both a comprehension that Indians are indeed different from non-Indians, and an awareness of specific Indian points of view. Larry was a mainstay at the Indian Center almost from its inception and demonstrated his understanding of Indian people in many ways. I was an inexperienced graduate student, whose previous knowledge of Indians had been garnered only from books and classes, and I demonstrated my ignorance daily. Undoubtedly my eagerness to learn helped people overlook my ignorance, and by making no claims to knowledge I minimized my vulnerability as a target.

Particularly important was my willingness to hear Indian critiques of white society and of whites in general without defensiveness. This was made easier because I often agreed with the substance of the charges, but sometimes I was verbally attacked personally and the motives for my presence were impugned. I defended myself when I felt that this was an appropriate response, but I always tried to take the other person's position seriously. Several encounters that began this way led to mutual respect, and even friendship. Those encounters also helped to validate my relationships with those who already trusted me to some extent.

The third factor facilitating Larry's and my acceptance was the limits that we each placed on our respective roles. We both avoided interfering with people and making claims for ourselves, we were self-effacing and, in my case, I refrained from prying into sensitive areas. Larry, as a former employee of the welfare department, had a better sense of what went into dealing with city agencies and officials and how to facilitate the task of finding services for Indian people than did most of the Indians who worked with the Indian Center. At no time, however, did he parade his knowledge or make others feel ignorant. Little by little, he taught the Indian leaders much of what he knew, without interfering with their decision-making roles.

In addition to the fact that interference from me would have violated Indian norms, it would also have gone against the canons of field research methodology. Accordingly, I tried hard to avoid giving unsolicited advice, even when I thought it was needed. Adhering to this Indian value of noninterference enhanced my acceptance, and demonstrated my confidence in the right of Indian people to make their own decisions. While my advice was occasionally sought and followed, I took a passive role at the Indian Center. To further avoid disruption, I rarely took notes or used a tape recorder in public. I avoided asking for information that would appear useless in the eyes of my informants. I felt that otherwise I would be labeled as just another prying researcher.

I discovered that two subjects, Indian medicine and Indian religion, generally were taboo for the most part. I was very careful about the kinds of questions that I asked about both topics, and I attended Indian ceremonies only when invited.

In time, Larry (especially) and I were occasionally included in references to "the Indians." Once several people said they were planning to make us Indians, and an Indian woman stated that she had been thinking of Larry as an Indian. I never made any claim of my own to "Indian" status, however, and neither did Larry. I am convinced that if either of us had we would not have been nearly as well-received. By "knowing our place," we were accepted as few non-Indians were, while paradoxically, whites with small but legitimate claims to actual Indian heritage were scorned because they made those claims without being involved in an Indian community.

One of my research goals was to identify and interview non-Indians, particularly those connected with public agencies or service institutions, who had extensive experience relating to Indians. Eventually, my focus came to rest on the health field, and after many interviews I discovered a handful of people in health-related roles who had developed bonds with Indians. I also discovered that their roles, although in some ways very different from mine and Larry's with respect to Indians, generally resembled ours in significant respects.

First and foremost, every physician and nurse who had felt successful in working with Indians and who, despite the small percentage of Indians in the city, could count a disproportionate number of Indian patients, characterized his or her relationship with Indian patients as more than strictly "professional." Each either recognized the need for a personal relationship with Indian patients, or genuinely enjoyed the opportunity to get to know Indian people. One young Indian woman commented about her white doctor: "He'll sit on the bed and talk to you just like one of the family."

These relationships did not occur overnight but, once made, were very strong. As a nurse from the chest clinic stated, "Indians are withdrawn and quiet until they get to know you. But I've been here since the Year One, and once they get to know you they really trust you, and some of them will almost take their drugs to please me now." The best known and most well-liked physician, as far as the Indians were concerned, was Dr. Thompson, a white pediatrician who had begun her involvement with Indians by holding clinics once a week on the Pottawatomi reservation. As her interest in Indians deepened and as more people came to trust her she became, in effect, *the* pediatrician for Indians. She also became an advocate for Indians, and succeeded in having a federally funded health screening program become available to all the Indian children in Prairie County for a year, even though other participants were more restricted geographically. When she moved away from the city in mid-1970, she was revered by virtually the entire Indian community--and no other non-Indian approached that status. Yet it had taken her more than two years of weekly pilgrimages to the reservation to *begin* to win that trust.

An indication of the strength of these relationships is the fact that once established, most Indians always come to the trusted doctor or nurse for medical help, regardless of the type of problem. One physician said former Indian patients still call him from 75 miles away. "They ask me who to go to if there is something in particular wrong." Other doctors reported the same pattern. A public health nurse who had worked with Indian families for five years said that she had spent a great deal of time with one family that subsequently moved out of the city. When they moved back and a son became ill the mother called on her with the explanation, "I couldn't think of any other nurse but you when I came back."

The second characteristic of these health care workers that aided their relationships with Indian patients is that they knew a lot about Indians--at least in comparison to the rest of the non-Indian population. Their interest in their patients had paid off in increased knowledge about Indians per se, with the result that they were able both to offer better service and to enhance the relationship in the eyes of their Indian patients. Said one woman of her doctor, "He's real interested in Indians and he's even been out to our Pow Wows." Another Indian woman had this to say about Dr. Thompson: "She really understood us. She could probe deeper than them other doctors. . .We hardly opened our mouths and she'd understand." A different white physician echoed the opinion that it was necessary to know the right questions to ask Indian patients, and to understand and adjust to their tendency to minimize pain. This man also displayed a surprising knowledge of Indian contributions to medicine, which undoubtedly raised his status in the eyes of his Indian patients. (Although Indian medical practices, which are intimately tied to Indian religion, were closely guarded secrets, the general lack of public awareness of Indian contributions to Euro-American medicine and of the efficacy of Indian modes of healing was a source of irritation to Indians generally).

I was unable to actually witness the interaction of physicians and patients, but I observed five well child clinics held by the health department for Indian children at an Indian Protestant mission church in Prairie City. Although the nurses at the clinic were not as experienced with Indian patients as two others whom I interviewed, they were either well-coached or else intuitively knew what to do. The informal, all-Indian setting and the assistance of a Pottawatomi nurse's aide also contributed to a relaxed and supportive atmosphere. The nurses established good rapport with the mothers and grandmothers who brought the children to the clinic, and they asked questions in a low-keyed manner. They also avoided the indiscretions toward Indians described above as characteristic of some non-Indians. No one, for example, criticized, patronized, or scolded the parents. Suggestions for improved childcare--e.g., in the children's diets--were made in a positive, relaxed, and friendly manner, and the parents responded amiably.

The gap that has been described in this article between the Indian community and the rest of the urban population has been fully recognized by many individuals within the Indian community. For many years, the informal role of "Indian caretaker"--helping other Indians get along in the city--had been filled by a few individuals who generally were more financially successful than their brethren and who were more attuned to the urban and Euro-American approach to problem-solving. Some were marginal to the Indian community themselves, to a degree, but wished to remain part of that community. They naturally and easily fell into the role of caretaker, which not only helped out other Indians, but gave them a measure of leadership status among both Indians and non-Indians. These caretakers were sought out for advice about welfare, jobs, housing, and similar matters, and often acted as advocates, translators, and facilitators on behalf of other Indians before the proper forums.

The value of the Indian caretaker role was also recognized by certain agency personnel within the city, and efforts were made in the late 1960's to institutionalize it on several fronts. The state employment office in Prairie City was apparently the first agency to hire an Indian for the specific purpose of serving other Indians, and an attempt was made to have at least one Indian person employed there at all times. A five-year health screening project for children recruited three Pottawatomi women to serve as volunteer outreach workers. One of these women was later employed by the city-county health department as a nurse's aide.

Another Indian woman worked with a program that prepared minority group members for apprenticeship within building trade unions, and a relatively large number of Indians entered this program.

The value of institutionalizing the caretaker role was also recognized within the Indian community, and resulted in the formation of the Indian Center of Prairie City, Inc., in 1969. As one caretaker and a founder of the Center stated, "We decided to get together to do what we'd been doin' anyway." The purpose of the Indian Center was succinctly expressed on another occasion by its president, who stated, "It's to help the (Indian) people help themselves. It serves as a go-between the people and existing agencies." For example, recognizing that an Indian setting is far more comfortable for Indian people than an agency office, Center leaders have encouraged agency personnel to hold appointments at the Center building.

An additional important function of the Indian Center has been its role as a focus for non-Indian groups, agencies, and individuals who desire some relationship with Indians in Prairie City. The Indian Center is an identifiable group with a physical headquarters where information about Indians may be found (e.g., for tourist and college classes), where Indian opinions on any subject may be solicited (e.g., for journalists and politicians), where information may be publicized to Indian people (e.g., notices of job openings), and where new avenues of interracial cooperation and mutual help may be explored. Indian public relations within Prairie City improved significantly after the establishment of the Center. At the same time, through their work at the Center, many Indians gained expertise in dealing with a wide range of non-Indian individuals, groups and agencies throughout the urban area.

The two final examples of positive bonds between Indians and non-Indians in Prairie City took place on a group level, rather than between individuals. Shortly after I left the field, an event occurred that upset many Indians in Prairie City. A local auditorium booked a performance of the Koshare Dancers, a group of whites who donned costumes and performed "authenic" Hopi Indian dances. Many of the dances were sacred to the Hopis, and most Prairie City Indians felt that for non-Indians to imitate these dances before a paying audience would be a profanation of Hopi religion--and as such an insult to the sensitivities of all Indians. The Indians tried to persuade the proprietors of the auditorium to cancel the engagement, but were refused. They then attempted to obtain a court injuction against the performance; again, they failed. Finally, they organized a demonstration that was held outside the auditorium before and during the dancing. During the demonstration, some of the younger, more activist Indians attempted to disrupt the performance and were arrested. Other Indians were embarrassed over the spectacle of a demonstration and refused to participate; one Pottawatomi woman resigned from the Indian Center board in protest against the picketing.

In all the excitement, however, an additional occurrence was noticed by the Indians. Their demonstration was quietly joined by a group of blacks, who thus affirmed their support of the Indian position about the dancing. This made a significant impression on the Indians; indeed, it evoked the most positive comments about blacks that I have heard in my association with Prairie City Indians. For once, they felt, blacks were not trying to manipulate the Indians for their own purposes, but were joining in an Indian action that had no visible payoff for the blacks. Blacks were thus affirming the Indian's right to be *Indians*, as well as symbolically suggesting the need for minority groups to stick together.

The most successful example of cooperation between Indians and non-Indians in Prairie City was the Beaver Hollow Indian Festival, which resulted from a joint project of the Indian Center and the Southside Presbyterian Church, an all-white church of less than 150 members. Apparently, the idea for the festival originated with the two men who coordinated it, who also worked together at the Veterans Administration Hospital--Vernon, a middleaged Citizen Band Pottawatomi, one of the Indian "caretakers," and Harry, a 45-year old active layman in the church. At the time, the church was attempting to find funding for the Indian Center at its denominational headquarters. Four years earlier, in 1967, a similar festival had occurred; that event, however, took place before the Indian Center was created, and was a less ambitious project.

The primary purpose of the occasion was to publicly celebrate Indian culture through a weekend of Indian singing and dancing. It was also variously seen as a way to promote interracial understanding, have fun, and raise money (to be divided between the Center and the church). Committees were formed, consisting of both Indians and whites, to generate publicity, sell tickets, and prepare the site. The most significant feature of the cooperative effort was that the bulk of the behind-the-scenes work was done by the church people, while most of the public attention was focused on the Indians. Furthermore, the preparation was carried out to the Indians' specifications.

Although less money was raised than had been hoped, in every other way the Beaver Hollow Indian Festival was a resounding success. A respectably large number of Indian dancers, including a few from other states, participated. The audiences were appreciative. A big dinner was prepared for the dancers on Saturday night by the church people, and on Sunday an elderly Kickapoo man who was still an active and exciting dancer was honored, as planned. I observed with interest and pleasure that the Indian-white interaction seemed smooth in every respect. Awkwardness was mitigated by the nature of the project: the goal was to accomplish a specific task. Through working side by side, Indians and whites became comfortable with each other, and personal relationships were established among the most active participants. The two coordinators worked effectively with each other and with their respective groups. Clearly, their personal relationship was one of the most important factors in the success of the venture.

CONCLUSION

The value of this study is limited in part by the nature of all case studies: they describe one or a few situations that may be relatively or entirely unique and that therefore are of limited use in discovering general characteristics of the broader subject under investigation. I suspect, however, that many of the factors discussed above are relevant to a broad range of settings, rural as well as urban, where Indians and non-Indians live or meet. They are offered, then, not only as the findings of one research project, but as possible hypotheses for many more.

Although I have emphasized the gap that exists between them, Indians and non-Indians are strikingly similar in several respects. Most people do not get along well with other folk who deny or denigrate the former's self-image. Thus Indians expect--demand--to be treated as *Indians*, not as whites, Chicanos, or "just another minority group." Few among us enjoy being sterotyped. The desire for identity, dignity, courtesy, and at least a measure of self-determination is universal.

The roadblocks are many to good relations between people-- or peoples--who are different from each other in significant respects. They are particularly formidable and hazardous when those who are involved are representatives of groups characterized by great power inequality or that see each other as threatening or competitive. Perhaps the surprising fact is that good relations exist at all, ever. Those of us who wish to make them more frequent and persistent may be more successful if we hold before us a paradox. Interracial bonds cannot begin without an acknowledgement that real, substantial, and frequently troublesome differences do indeed exist. That is the paradox: by fully exploring our differences we discover our commom humanity.

FOOTNOTES

1. Indian-white relations are the focal point of the article but I do touch on the relationships of Indians with blacks and Chicanos. The term "non-Indian" is sometimes used, not to obscure differences among these groups but as a convenient way of distinguishing between Indians and groups they regard as "others."

SOURCES

C. Hoy Steele, *American Indians and Urban Life: A Community Study*, Ph.D. dissertation, Department of American Studies, University of Kansas, Lawrence, Kansas, 1972.

──────────────────,"The acculturation/assimilation model in urban Indian studies: a critique." Pp. 305-314 in Norman R. Yetman and C. Hoy Steele (eds.), *Majority and Minority: The Dynamics of Racial and Ethnic Relations*, 2nd. ed., Boston: Allyn and Bacon, 1975.

INTRODUCTION TO PART TWO

BONDS FOR EFFECTING POLITICAL AND SOCIAL ACTION

Each of the selections to follow deal with interracial efforts to effect political and social change. The goal is the same--securing the rights of black and ultimately all Americans--but the groups and coalitions of groups vary. The range includes an active, day-by-day interacting interracial CORE group of civil rights days, as well as coalitions of separate black and white organizations. The coalition process can be effectively used by groups which are part of the official governing structures as well as by citizen activist groups. It is also a type of bonding that brings members of separate groups together over specific issues.

Priscilla Chenoweth's personal reflections on her work with a New Jersey CORE chapter reveals the unanticipated gains derived by white individuals from such participation. In jointly assessing strategy and tactics to be pursued, white members were forced to face the deficiencies of their experience and to hone their sensitivities in the area of race; to learn how to translate their good intentions into successful achievement. In the process of such growth, Chenoweth found her personal life tremendously enriched, and her commitment to interracial activity strengthened. One wonders how the minority person felt in the role of teacher and whether the rewards of helping to develop more humanistic whites justified the effort. Chenoweth recognizes the objections of some blacks to this role and acknowledges her appreciation of those who guided her.

Introduction to Part Two

Next, the director of the Nashville Metropolitan Human Relations Commission, Fred Cloud, discusses community issues in which his group was able to play a successful role. Without minimizing racial differences, and by assessing the type of contribution specific organizations and individuals could make, Cloud and the commission were able to create effective community coalitions. The aims, strategies and timing of these efforts bear examination by those seriously involved in social action. As in the case of many of the selections in this book, Cloud describes the events from the vantage point of his own role. He was not asked to discuss the "ups and downs" of Commission work, but rather its victories.

The CORE chapter depicted by Chenoweth was an interracial civil rights organization. Such groups declined in number with the growth of the Black Power movement in the late 1960's. Blacks, for once, were openly expressing their inability to trust most whites. Yet, as indicated in our general introduction, even then a number of uneasy black-white coalitions developed. Guida West, who herself was active in a "twin-track" welfare rights group, studied several twin-tracks that sprang to life briefly and at approximately the same historical moment. These groups were racially separate and their cooperation was based on the leadership of the black group. The reader may want to ask such questions as: What were the similar rules of the game developed in these different cases of allied black and white groups? Did they succeed in their attempts to reverse the usual power relationships between the races?

4

BLACK AND WHITE TOGETHER: A TIME TO REMEMBER

By

Priscilla Read Chenoweth

During the early 1960's I was vice chairman of an active, integrated CORE chapter that functioned in the "black and white together" spirit of our anthem, "We Shall Overcome." The sixties seem to have acquired a bad name these days, but I recall a time of worthwhile work and comradeship and some achievements.

While I grew up in a pleasant, tree-lined section of Flatbush, in Brooklyn, the only black people I ever saw there were a middle-aged couple who superintended an apartment building on our block. George--and it is, of course, significant that I, a child, knew him as "George"--tended the furnace in the three-family house in which my family lived. My mother, who was originally Swedish, made a point of describing him as a "gentleman," and he was. He and his wife once kindly invited my two sisters and me to their home to see his terrier's puppies. I remember being enthralled by the puppies, but otherwise feeling awkward. However, almost all human encounters made me feel awkward then.

My mother had some friends who were Ba'hai's, and I have a dim recollection of going to some Ba'hai affairs, which were integrated; George Schuyler, the journalist, and his daughter Phillipa, the pianist, were there and I heard her play--if memory does not serve me false.

We belonged to the All Souls Universalist Church on Ocean Avenue. It was all white. A black boy was a member of the Boy Scout troop there for a while and the minister referred to him from the pulpit as "the chocolate drop." Once a black couple came to a service and the minister and deacons prided themselves on how tactfully--and successfully--they had suggested that they might be "happier elsewhere." This was about 1938. I like to think that I felt the same rage then as I do now, but I can't be sure.

I do know that my father, who despised that minister, loathed all forms of prejudice. He was originally a farm boy from Swanzie, New Hampshire, of an old Yankee family, mainly farmers. His mother was either a niece or a cousin of Horace Mann (I never got that straight) and I gathered from things Papa said that there was a strong abolitionist tradition in the family. I like to believe this, too. He went to Harvard on a scholarship and was in the same class as Franklin D. Roosevelt, although they moved in entirely different circles. There is an apocryphal story about my father that he refused his degree because of a Jim Crow incident. Whether the story is true or not, it says something about him that it was told at all. He was fifty-one when I was born, and I never did know him as well as I would have liked.

There were no black students at P.S. 152, which I attended, and hardly any at Erasmus Hall High School. My big breakout from the WASP world of All Souls was into the world of my Jewish classmates. I had been appalled at the revelations of the Nazi death camps and was aware of the horrors of anti-Semitism, but until I was fifteen I felt, despite some school friendships, very conscious of and alien from Jews and Jewishness. (This was very true of the All Souls congregation; Protestants were a minority in Flatbush and they acted like a beleaguered one.)

At Erasmus, after I had spent an unhappy freshman year palling around with girls I didn't really like just because they were WASPs (I hate that term but must admit it is useful) I was fortunate enough to be befriended by a number of Jewish kids. Scales fell from my eyes and I began to enjoy more of the richness of the world around me.

It was then that I gave up my parents' Republicanism and started exploring what was meant by Socialism. My closest friends came from American Labor Party backgrounds. Their parents had become communists for the best of reasons, truly believing in equality, peace and justice, and had later, after the Moscow purge trials, the Hitler-Stalin pact and the Russian invasion of Finland, either left the Party heartbroken or closed their minds and stayed because they couldn't bear to know the truth. (Some of them would finally leave, after the existence of the slave labor camps was revealed and then the uprisings in Hungary and Czechoslovakia crushed.)

I didn't know all of this about Russia then. I was skeptical about "our faithful ally"; when I was fifteen World War II had just ended and the American propaganda mills during the war glossed over any little faults. I don't think I realized then that there *were* anti-communist socialists; I was just groping my way.

When I was sixteen, I was invited by a friend, who was also groping, to go with a group of Quakers on a lobbying weekend in Washington. Bayard Rustin was there, and gave a talk. It wasn't about civil rights (I think it was about the Marshall Plan) but the whole weekend was an education--more, a revelation--in civil rights to me. Simply meeting Bayard (we are old friends now) was an education in civil rights. There were black students in the group, from Virginia, Maryland and North Carolina, and they told me about Jim Crow--all about Jim Crow. I had had no idea. Literally, no idea.

Segregation was brought home to me by the fact that the only place we could eat in Washington, the only non-segregated restaurant, was the cafeteria in the Supreme Court building. I always had a kindly feeling for the Supreme Court after that.

My first day-to-day interracial friendships were formed at college. Although there weren't very many black students there then, Oberlin is proud of the fact that it was founded as an integrated college--the first in America--and so was I. There was an NAACP chapter on campus, which I joined. I don't recall our being particularly active, but we did boycott a racist restaurant in town, which gave us a certain feeling of camaraderie. I occasionally dated two black students, one from Liberia, one from Cleveland (and yearned after a third who never asked me out). I sometimes went to parties with them where there was only one other white; he was half of an interracial couple that was well known and liked on campus; if I recall correctly they eventually married. The point here is that this was accepted quite matter-of-factly at Oberlin.

The most important thing politically that happened to me at Oberlin was that I met some students who belonged to the Independent Socialist League, a small group of democratic, anti-totalitarian socialists. When I transferred after two years to the University of Chicago, I had introductions to the members there, among them my future husband, Don (a WASP like me). I had found my political home.

The ISL's chairman, Max Schactman, had been one of those who followed Trotsky out of the Communist Party and formed the Socialist Workers Party (the parent organization of the Young Socialist Alliance, active today). Opposed to the increasing repression in the Soviet Union, Schactman and a number of others subsequently broke with the SWP and its position of basic support for what it insisted on still considering a "workers' state" and, therefore, whatever its faults, superior per se to any capitalist country. The ISL was formed and later merged with the Socialist Party of Eugene Debs and Norman Thomas, presently known as the Social Democrats, USA. Bayard Rustin is now the chairman, and A. Philip Randolph is an honorary chairman. As I said, this is my political home and, among my comrades, interracial relationships are taken for granted.

My husband and I moved back to New York in 1951 and, after he had served as national director of the ISL's youth group for two years while I worked in a factory to support us, he became a typographer, our first child was born, and I became a full-time mother. In various ways our paths crossed with Bayard's and the better I got to know him the more impressed I was.

When our third child was born, we were living in a one-bedroom garden apartment in Queens. Don and I had saved what seemed to us to be an enormous amount, and started looking for a house. It never occurred to us at first to leave New York City, but the only houses available were being sold for much more than we had. We had to go where FHA mortgage money was available: either Long Island or New Jersey. We chose Metuchen (pop. approximately 14,000), New Jersey and thus became part of the "white flight" from the city, a term about which I am therefore, somewhat skeptical.

Two black fellow socialists, Norman and Velma Hill, had

become close friends of ours and spent occasional weekends at our new house. They were both working for the Congress of Racial Equality and we had many long discussions about civil rights goals, strategy and tactics.

It must have been the spring of 1961 when I heard that a Metuchen-Edison Racial Relations Council was being formed, the prime movers being members of the local Presbyterian church. I called, expressed an interest, attended the early organizational meetings and was given the responsibility of forming an Employment Committee. At one of those early organizational meetings, a big, middle-aged black man seated behind me made what I considered a telling point (I wish I could remember what it was, but I can't, and neither can he.) I turned around and smiled and caught his eye, and thus began a long partnership in civil rights activity and an enduring friendship with Bill.

Bill Williams had been a union organizer in the South in the thirties and a Marine combat sergeant in the Pacific during World War II. When we walked some of our hairier picket lines, even though CORE members were dedicated to non-violence, it was reassuring to know he was there. But I am getting ahead of my story.

Bill and his wife and Doris Wynn, a black trade unionist with the IUE, chose to work with the Employment Committee and recruited a number of their friends. Our first project was to interview all the storekeepers in Metuchen and discuss hiring policies. (This was, remember, before anti-discrimination laws had been passed.) The expressed attitude was good and we moved on to the Menlo Park shopping center in Edison. Again, we got a favorable reception. This was all very well, but a few jobs in a few stores was, we felt, pretty small potatoes. We took a look at the major employers and pretty well determined that, on the whole, Gulton Industries in Metuchen and Ford and Revlon in Edison were hiring on an equality basis. More and more the talk turned to Johnson and Johnson, the biggest employer in Middlesex County and the only big corporation with its headquarters here. Every black member of the committee either had had or knew of an experience that pointed to a discriminatory hiring practice. Certainly, from what we were able to determine, there were too few black employees at J & J.

Part of the reason for this went quite far back, and was true of many large companies. Whenever labor was scarce at the end of the nineteenth and beginning of the twentieth century, companies would not turn to the black labor force in the South, but went recruiting in Europe. J&J had traditionally recruited in Hungary, and Middlesex County, particularly New Brunswick, has one of the largest concentrations of Hungarian-Americans in the country. In the sixties, when there was no more recruiting in Hungary itself, job vacancies were usually filled by grapevine from the Hungarian-American community.

We wrote to J&J, requesting a meeting, but received no response, and there didn't seem to be anything we could do. We were, after all, just a committee of the Metuchen-Edison Council. Not only was J&J outside our jurisdiction, as it were, but the rest of the Council was nervously conservative. (When some of us joined a perfectly respectable picket line outside Woolworth's in another town in support of Martin Luther King, many of the members were scandalized.)

So it seemed logical for me to suggest to the Employment Committee members that we ask Norman and Velma to come and discuss the possibility of forming a CORE chapter. And we did, and they did, and Middlesex-Union County CORE was started. The chairman was Bob Richardson, then chief steward of the UAW at the Ford plant. Later, as we grew, we divided into a Union County and a Middlesex County CORE and Bill Williams became chairman of Middlesex. I was vice chair.

The chapter was about half black and half white. It would be foolish to say that there were no interracial problems, that there was no insensitivity on the part of whites or resentments on the part of blacks or misunderstandings on the part of both, but we dealt with them; we discussed and analyzed and, for the most part, solved the problems that arose.

This was mainly thanks to Norman and Velma. Completely oriented to problem solving, dedicated to the integrationist point of view, and having no hang-ups themselves about whites and working with whites, they were able to articulate and resolve black/white problems. Of course, they rarely had a chance to do so with our chapter, being busy national CORE functionaries (Norman became program director of the organization), but they had gotten us started and their influence remained. And since they were close friends, Don and I felt free to call them for advice.

There had been some talk of my being the chairperson of CORE. I was probably the most active member--not working or being pregnant, and I enjoyed the work involved. However, I felt that it was inappropriate for a white to be the head of a CORE chapter. I had no compunction about saying that I *would* be glad to accept the vice chairmanship.

Earlier, I mentioned our interviewing local storekeepers. We did that in teams of one black and one white. This was a conscious, considered decision that, we felt, paid off. We weren't dealing with philosophical questions about whether people *should* react in such-and-such a way; we were working to overcome discrimination against blacks in employment and, in the circumstances, the interracial team approach worked best. It also had the side benefit of creating closer relationships between blacks and whites in the group.

It was mainly the blacks in the chapter who educated the whites, particularly the sensitive and articulate Bill Williams. They had had to be conscious of their relationships with whites all their lives. Most of the white members were certainly well-intentioned but, until their CORE experience, had not had, or thought very much about, relationships with blacks--the "invisible man" syndrome. I read a remark once by a black college student, asked why blacks had become so separatist on college campuses, to the effect that he was tired of being the first black acquaintance for so many whites and having to be the teacher for each one he met. I am grateful to my black friends for their patience.

I have heard, and can well believe it, that a lot of the impetus for black separatism came from a reaction to some of the whites who entered into the civil rights movement with an appalling degree of insensitivity and arrogance. For example, at one time, a group of Rutgers students, all white, attempted to organize a CORE chapter in opposition to ours. They were very "radical" and scorned us for what they considered our conservative ways, but it did seem to belie their professed concerns to see them try to cut down some of our long-time black leaders. They didn't succeed.

However, although I may understand some of the reasons

for the separatist creed, I disagree with it. No matter how tough the going, integration is a necessary goal. In the social democratic movement, we have not been swayed (as too many liberals have) to abandon our goal or lose faith in the possibility of its attainment.

As for my leadership role in CORE, I think that it came about because--as everyone in the chapter knew--my mentors were black. It wasn't a case of coming in saying, "whitey knows best." The people I looked to for leadership were the Hills, and Ernest Rice McKinney and Bayard Rustin and, through them, the great A. Philip Randolph himself. Moreover, Don and I made clear we were not being altruistic do-gooders. We strongly believe that the country's future depends in large part on how, and how well, it deals with the problems of black Americans. Therefore we had, and have, a healthy concern for ourselves and our children. Whites who came into the civil rights movement feeling that they were doing blacks a favor could be a pain in the neck.

We had a lot of good times. Don and I often went to dances where we were the only whites, many of them sponsored by the Perth Amboy NAACP as fund raisers. We developed close friendships with some black couples we met because of CORE and went to a lot of parties and played a lot of pinochle. And our children benefited from having black friends.

As for achievements--well, the civil rights bills of 1964 and 1965 were passed, and we liked to feel that we were part of the large national effort that was responsible for this. We participated in other national or regional CORE efforts, like the White Tower restaurants project. And when we felt strong enough and experienced enough, we wrote to J & J again. This time, we said that we would throw up a picket line or two if they wouldn't meet with us; they met with us.

J & J has really changed. Today, it has many minority workers, including a number of blacks in managerial positions, and it was instrumental in forming a very successful organization called Project Action, which reaches out to bring jobs and minority workers in the country together. To what extent were we responsible for this change? It's hard to say, but those many long meetings must have had some effect. The same with New Jersey Bell. It was very basic, nitty-gritty stuff, those meetings, like explaining that it had been against the law in slave states to teach blacks to read.

We--mainly Bill Williams and I--were very actively involved in the March on Trenton in October, 1963. It was a coalition effort, like the March on Washington, which inspired it, and we were mainly pressing for the enactment of open housing and other anti-discrimination legislation. I'll never forget that day, a beautiful Indian sumer day. A committee, which I was on, met with Governor (now Chief Justice) Richard J. Hughes to present our demands. He supported our legislative goals, so it was to some extent just a formality, but it was very important to sit down and discuss these matters with him.

We had distributed the call for the march as widely as possible and hoped for the best. People were to assemble at the railroad station in Trenton and march up West State Street to the mall at 4 p.m. Our meeting with the Governor started at 3:30. By 4:15 there was no sign of a parade past the State House and I began to get nervous thinking that no one had come. Excusing myself, I went outside and saw--beautiful to behold--Bayard walking in the middle of the street with thousands of people (later estimated as between 17,000 and 25,000) behind him. It was a great day. To what extent the march was responsible for the fact that the legislation was subsequently passed, I don't know, but it can't have hurt.

The times have changed. When major civil rights legislation was passed, the emphasis shifted to economic problems, and *they* can only be solved in a broader political framework of setting goals for the betterment of *all* disadvantaged Americans. We who were active before have to get active again, and some of us have been talking about this and how to go about influencing the electoral process to that end. One thing is for sure. Ever since I got my wits about me, it has been black and white together, and it always will be...

5

WORKING TOGETHER FOR SOCIAL CHANGE

By

Fred Cloud

The concept of change is no new thing: one of the pre-Socratic philosophers remarked, "You can't step into the same stream twice." But Alvin Toffler and others have made us aware that the rate and magnitude of change in our time is mind-boggling. As human relations workers in a time of constant change we have to be sensitive to, and responsive to, changes in intergroup relations. Further, we have to develop strategies appropriate for the changed circumstances.

Many of the changes that confront us in America today are unplanned. Our concern is to focus on those areas where planned change is possible. Here I will describe some activities in one southern city (Nashville, Tennessee) over the decade 1965-1975 by blacks and whites working together to effect some specific social changes. They are described from the vantage point of a staff member of the Metropolitan Human Relations Commission who was on the scene and involved in all of the ventures. There are undoubtedly some blind spots in the author's perception of what was happening. Even so, it is offered as one viewpoint for whatever insight it might provide the reader.

The basic commitment of the Commission during the past decade was first, *to make structural changes* that would open the door of opportunity for blacks in Nashville and secure fair treatment for them at the hands of both government and the private sector; and second, to provide supportive services that would encourage the formation of attitudes supportive of the new structural relationships. There were some successes and some failures.

Basically, it was an uphill road--every day. Sisyphus sets the style for human relations workers!

When the status quo is shafting blacks in several ways, how can that status quo be changed? Our experience underlines the accuracy of Kurt Lewin's force field analysis. He contends that "change can be viewed as a result of the shifting of the balance of forces that are working in opposite directions and maintaining a dynamic equilibrium or the status quo. This balance can be altered by increasing the forces that are exerting pressure on one side, by reducing the pressures of the forces on the other side, or by a combination of the two."

That analysis was borne out in the effort to secure Nashville's first Fair Employment Ordinances, an effort begun in July, 1967, and completed one year later. What were the contending forces? The positive pressures for change included the 1964 Civil Rights Act and blacks' rising tide of dissatisfaction with discrimination in employment. The pressure for maintaining the status quo came from racist attitudes of white employers and the desire to keep wages low and profits high. How could one tip the balance in favor of new Fair Employment laws and practices?

We set out both to increase the pressure for change and to reduce the resistance to change. First, we set about the task of organizing the community to press for change. Representatives of all the groups--black and white--that might favor fair employment were contacted and then convened. They organized as Citizens for Fair Employment, elected their own officers, and mapped out a strategy for action. That strategy included having *each* group in the coalition draft its own statement for the press, calling for Fair Employment laws, and releasing the statements one-per-week, so as to keep the issue before the public and--hopefully--to get a snowball effect.

Meanwhile, the Human Relations Commission gathered Fair Employment laws from other cities, studied them and drafted proposed ordinances. The Commission began negotiating with the Metropolitan Council to secure passage of the ordinances. Simultaneously, the Commission began meeting with the Chamber of Commerce, pointing out that it would be a forward step for Nashville to have enforceable Fair Employment laws. After seven months of pushing and persuading, the Council passed the ordinances, the Mayor signed them, and the Human Relations

Commission began enforcing them. Nashville became the second southern city (after Louisville, Kentucky) to have such laws.

Reflecting on that experience, one began to see the usefulness of a model for planned social change. One that was found useful and illuminating is Christopher Sower's five-stage model, as described in Lyle E. Schaller's book, *The Change Agent:*
1. Focusing discontent with the status quo.
2. Formation of an initiating group.
3. Developing a supporting group.
4. Establishing a group to carry out the plans, and mobilizing community resources.
5. Institutionalizing or freezing the new structure or level of performance.

This model was applied to the relationship that existed between Nashville blacks and the police.

In 1967 and 1968, as a result of police/black confrontations, especially following the assassination of Dr. Martin Luther King, Jr., many blacks in Nashville filed complaints with the Human Relations Commission, alleging mistreatment at the hands of the police. The first step for social change--discontent with the status quo--was there in full force.

The Commission saw this as a ripe moment to act. It saw itself as the initiating group; so it held public hearings to call this injustice to the attention of the total community. Then it urged the Mayor and the Chief of Police to institute two basic measures: human relations training for all policemen and psychological screening of all applicants for the police department. The strong public pressure at that time undoubtedly helped the Mayor and the Chief of Police to say "yes" to both these measures.

The Commission then pulled together a group of twenty black and white social scientists, psychologists, and psychiatrists to develop the training design. A grant was secured from the U. S. Department of Justice to fund the initial training. The entire Police Department, from Chief to rookie, participated in this Human Relations training.

At the conclusion of the first cycle of training, the Police Department wrote the training and screening program into its budget. Now, the training is done on a contractual basis by the Center for Community Studies, and the screening is done by the Vanderbilt University Department of Psychiatry. Thus, we see that Sower's five-stage model of planned change actually describes what happened in this instance.

In the late 1960's it was evident to the Commission that Nashville's communications media were failing to communicate with a substantial segment of the population--the 19.2 per cent who were black. The black community saw Nashville's newspapers, television stations, and radio stations as blind and uncaring regarding local conditions that affected blacks. They felt excluded from the press, that news of the black community was not honestly or adequately covered, and that blacks were discriminated against in employment by the media.

On the initiative of the Human Relations Commission, a group of black and white leaders in media and community relations were brought together. After extended planning sessions, they projected a "Consultation on Mass Media and Race Relations." Funding was secured from a private foundation and from the Community Relations Service of the Justice Department.

One of the realities which the Committee had to face was that the working press could not be expected to respond to the anticipated demands of the public unless they were free to do so. This freedom could only come as a result of a desire for change on the part of the owners of mass media. Another reality was the knowledge that none of the Committee members had the kind of entrée with the media owners which could assure their cooperation. One of the Committee members knew of one man in Nashville who could assure maximum cooperation among the owners. He set up a meeting in his office between the Committee and David K. Wilson, after which Wilson agreed to host a private luncheon for all of the media owners. Thirty owners and managers attended. Carl Rowan, guest speaker, challenged the group of executives to consider some alternative ways of achieving their goals in news coverage.

After these top level executives had been convinced that a problem existed, and that the problem lay at their doors, the next step was simple. Second and third echelon personnel were delegated to attend the Consultation plenary sessions and to cooperate with the Program Committee. About 110 persons participated in this Consultation, on May 21-22, 1969.

Perhaps, the single most effective part of the program was

two hours of "Community Feedback". This was a series of candid taped interviews with citizens, on their attitudes toward news media. The candor of these comments sparked a great deal of discussion in which hostility among the delegates--community as well as media representatives--was revealed. Earlier talks had generally been tempered with consideration for variance in perception and opinion. Apparently the taped interviews, which were extremely hostile toward media, especially newspapers, laid bare nerve ends and set the stage for a more honest exchange. It became obvious that the stated goals of media were in conflict with what the community perceived as their purpose. Media leaders were forced to acknowledge and examine specific cases in which they did not convey the message that they had intended. Community participants were forced to assume a greater role in improving the quality of news coverage through cooperative efforts.

Following the consultation, the Human Relations Committee published a 32-page printed report of the Consultation, *Mass Media and Race Relations.* This report made several recommendations, including: continuation of the dialogue begun in the Consultation, and the launching of an all-out recruitment effort among the colleges and universities in Nashville for black employees by individual newspapers, radio and TV stations. Further, publishers and producers were urged to assign black reporters to present news objectively and also to do in-depth reporting which would include community feelings and problems.

This Consultation had varied and far-reaching results. Following it, a number of black reporters were hired by the newspapers, as well as by radio and TV stations. It also had unanticipated "spin-offs"--results that were good but that were not originally envisioned by the planning committee: First, in 1970 a news media workshop was held at Tennessee State University on "Means of Communicating Issues in the Community." At this workshop, blacks were trained in writing that would get their organization's message to the community through the news media. Second, a Middle Tennessee Communications Coalition was formed to monitor radio and TV stations for fairness and adequacy of coverage of news of the black community. This coalition used the FCC license-review procedure to convince the stations to make positive changes.

Social changes, when they come, often come in "chains" or in "clusters." By being alert to what's happening, the Human Relations worker (in his role as a change agent) can help the changes along. However, it's important to recognize that the worker's relationship to the various change efforts will differ: sometimes one might be the initiator, at other times a supporter. In the instance described above, the black community took an increasing degree of initiative and leadership.

Earlier it was mentioned that "discontent with the status quo" is the first step or stage in planned social change. Sometimes that discontent is sharply focused by an incident, such as the shooting of a black youth by the police. Such an incident occurred in Nashville in 1971. In response to public outcry, the Council passed a resolution calling on the Human Relations Commission to make a study of "Reasons Why the Poor are Alienated From the Government."

The Commission accepted the challenge. It drafted a proposal and secured funding from the National Institute of Mental Health to underwrite the study. The black community and representatives of the poor were involved in this from the very outset. For example, the presidents of the Welfare Rights Organization, the Tenant's Rights Organization, and similar groups were retained as consultants along with some scholars from the universities. In carrying out the study, community residents were trained and hired as interviewers.

When the findings were in hand, printed copies of the report were given to all the black community organizations, with the recommendation that they press for the needed changes indicated in the report. The findings were presented to the Metropolitan Council, to the Mayor, to department heads of the city government, and to the media. In addition to newspaper coverage, the report was the subject of a thirty-minute TV special and a radio talk-show.

The above is spelled out because we are convinced that reports can be a leverage for social change when there is adequate follow-through. If simply presented to a city official, they probably will gather dust. But since the data is public, once released, it can be used to precipitate specific social changes. For example, one recommendation that grew out of the "Alienation" study was to have walking patrolmen in high-density neighborhoods. Several months later, after follow-up discussions between the Commission's staff and the police chief, this recommendation was implemented.

At the outset, we mentioned our commitment to make structural changes that will open the door of opportunity for blacks and women in Nashville. A major new step toward equal employment opportunity in Nashville was the adoption during 1974 of an Affirmative Action Plan for the entire Metropolitan Government. This was the work of a committee, chaired by the author. We insisted that the committee should have representation from the black community, as well as female members; this was done. The committee secured plans from various cities across America that had developed Affirmative Action plans and studied these carefully. It also secured guidelines from the Equal Employment Opportunity Commission.

Several drafts of the plan for Metro were developed, and heads of departments were given opportunity to make input as it was developed. Finally, the Affirmative Action Plan became effective on July 1, 1974, through an Executive Order issued by the Mayor.

We see *implementation* as the key to the effectiveness of this plan. And that involves black community organizations in an integral way: there are thirty-one referral agencies sending applicants to the government for possible hiring. Also, the plan requires community representation on the Committee that monitors *results* of the plan.

There is no "End" to the story of working together for social change. We have learned some useful things as we have lived through the experiences. As Ivan D. Illich says in *Celebration of Awareness;* "The change which has to be brought about can only be lived. We cannot plan our way to humanity. Each one of us and each of the groups with which we live and work must become a model of the era we desire to create."

SOURCES

Ivan D. Illich, *Celebration of Awareness,* Garden City: Doubleday Anchor Book, 1971.

Nashville Human Relations Commission, *Mass Media and Race Relations,* Report of a Consultation, May 21-22, 1969, Nashville, Tennessee.

Lyle E. Schaller, *The Change Agent,* Abingdon Press, 1972.

6

TWIN TRACK COALITIONS IN THE BLACK POWER MOVEMENT*

by

Guida West

The general frustrations of the civil rights movement, the advent of the "War on Poverty," and the eruption of urban disorders across the country in the mid-sixties, all contributed to the emergence of local as well as national black power movement organizations. The increasing demands among some of the more militant civil rights leaders that white allies be excluded from the black movement created a "pool" of unattached white liberals as well as disenchanted black leaders who continued to support the strategies of integration along with the newer goals of community organization and power.

The ideas of "maximum feasible participation" of the poor and organizing inner city communities, promoted by the Equal Opportunity Act of 1964, converged with those of the rising black power movement. The implementation of these principles helped provide the stimulus for the formation of independent black power movement organizations in the inner cities--organizations which lacked certification by the traditional black establishment.

Separation from whites and from traditional black leadership created the problem of finding alternative sources of support. While independence from whites was a cherished ideal, lack of resources within the black community mandated that assistance be sought from others. Blacks perceived a high risk in this

*In addition to sources cited at the end, this selection is based upon: interviews with many leaders, newspaper and newsletter articles, unpublished documents, correspondence and other information obtained from organizational files.

relationship--the potential of dominance by the more powerful whites. Necessity led to new types of alliances, which were not integrated but "parallel." These were "twin-track" coalitions, so labeled by this writer.

This type of alliance between blacks and whites recognizes both the independence and self-identity of the minority-power group as well as the advantages of support on specific issues from white "Friends" of the group. Such were some that appeared in different parts of the country: FIGHT and Friends of FIGHT, Black Peoples Unity Movement and the Friends of the BPUM, the Boston United Front and the Fund for Negro Urban Development, and the Black Panther Party and the Friends of the Panthers.

The groups were separate, the minority "track" was salient; there were linkages (visible or non-visible) for exchange of resources. The implicit "trade-off" in these coalitions was white resources "with no strings" in exchange for participation as a "Friend" in an "exclusive" black movement. In this new model, the unlike-power partners were not assumed to be equal within the alliance; blacks were the leaders and whites, the followers. Within the program environment the roles found in every-day social reality were reversed. While their strategies and tactics might differ, the independent partners shared the same goals.

The reason for the coalition was to combine resources-- cooperate--to achieve mutually-desired objectives. Generally this required dual strategies: mobilizing resources among peers and responding to the needs of one's non-peer partner. White "friends" had to choose between directing funds and resources to the black organization, or investing them in further mobilization of white support. The competition for scarce resources created serious conflicts when both strategies were combined. Where only support of the minority track was used, the passive and subordinate roles required of white supporters caused strain and schism. Nonetheless, these coalitions provided needed resources for black groups and the benefits of participation for white liberals while they functioned.

As the black urban poor increased demands for their rights, and the national mood became more hostile, some white liberal supporters began to drop by the wayside. Competitive movements were also emerging, such as the anti-war movement, women's liberation, and the ecology and environmental movements. For whites caught in the vacuum left by the changing civil rights struggle of the late sixties, these new causes provided an alternative: to continue alliances with blacks or to move into organizations that were predominantly white-oriented and dominated. This leads us into the story of some who chose to stay, trying to maintain and strengthen the interracial bonds between the blacks and whites in this country.

This essay examines the origins, structures, and consequences of four twin-track coalitions in the black power movements of Rochester (N.Y.), Camden (N.J.), Boston and Baltimore.

Rochester, New York: FIGHT and Friends of FIGHT

In the summer of 1964, Rochester was jolted into a racial crisis as riots ravaged parts of the city. The riots were attributed mainly "to the absence of power organization in the ghetto." The solution, according to some black and white liberal clergymen, was to create a viable organization in the black community of Rochester.

At the request of black clergymen, the predominately white Board of Urban Ministry (an almost autonomous arm of the Rochester Council of Churches), called in Saul Alinsky, the widely recognized radical white organizer of the black ghetto in Chicago. Hired for a period of two years (later extended for an additional year) by the major Protestant denominations to create an organization to empower the blacks in Rochester, Alinsky and his Rochester organizer, Ed Chambers, formed the black power organization called FIGHT (Freedom, Integration, God, Honor-Today) in June 1965. FIGHT, during its first convention and a major floor fight, changed its acronym to stand for Freedom, INDEPENDENCE, God, Honor-Today, reflecting more accurately the "separatist" nature of its structure and philosophy. Shortly afterwards, Chambers and Alinsky were confronted with an additional task: the reorganization of the white liberals who wanted a continuing role in the movement organization of the blacks.

Informed by Herbert White, Director of the Board of Urban Ministry, that a large number of "young and restless whites" were seeking a role in the new militant and "exclusive" black organization, Alinsky stated that he would like to try a new experiment: "setting up a white sister organization" parallel to FIGHT, namely Friends of FIGHT.

Its goals were the same as FIGHT's; its membership and leaders, however, were all white, upper middle-class, predominantly male, young and professional. The Twin-track structure was clearly one of separate but inter-dependent groups: blacks supported by white middle-class liberals. Both "tracks" were predominantly male-led and male-dominated. The two groups functioned not only independently, but jointly on issues identified by FIGHT. As one charter member of the Friends of FIGHT noted: "the whites and blacks were *apart but more together* than any integrated group...(emphasis mine)."

While this new structural relationship, initially at least, met the needs of both the blacks and the whites, leaders of the black "track" were wary of the risks involved in this coalition with a more powerful ally. For Alinsky, the architect of the "twin-track" coalition (although the term was never used by him, to my knowledge) this alliance between two unequal-power groups was designed with the safeguard of "separation" and controlled interaction between the two, to preclude the whites from "swallowing up" the black organization. Partially because the whites had played such a major role in proposing and underwriting the cost of Alinsky's coming to Rochester, the Reverend Florence, FIGHT's leader stated unequivocally that, "FIGHT would be doomed if any white man told it what to do." The need for a coalition between blacks and whites was evident to both sides, each of which perceived real "payoffs" in the relationship.

Common goals were to be achieved separately, but in partnership with each other. The organizations were mutually exclusive in terms of members, leaders, and finances. Final decisions on policy and tactics, however, had to be approved by FIGHT. Interaction was limited. Hence, within this local twin-track coalition, the usual roles were reversed: blacks led; whites followed. FIGHT set the agenda and the Friends responded. According to a story in the Newark Evening News, on May 6, 1969:

> The idea was to keep FIGHT all black, not to water it down as a sort of integrated "human relations" committee...The Friends were mostly middle-class, professional whites, but just as militant and abrasive, and our purpose was to assist

FIGHT in the white community, where FIGHT couldn't go. If FIGHT upset Rochester, the Friends of FIGHT practically made them drop their teeth. The key was that the whites were willing to take direction from the blacks--and this is what white Rochester couldn't understand.

While there were risks involved for the blacks in this new alliance, there were also dangers for the whites. Externally, they were highly criticized in the local press as "agitators." Internally, the new passive and subordinate role for white male professional leaders was costly and frustrating. Despite these strains, the coalition continued for over two years.

Its major cooperative venture was a nationally publicized confrontation with Eastman Kodak, whose headquarters were in Rochester. Two results of the black-white cooperation in this conflict were the eventual opening up of some jobs for blacks, and the establishment by the black community of its own manufacturing plant (FIGHTON) in cooperation with the U.S. Department of Labor and the Xerox Corporation. FIGHT selected workers to manage the new factory, with Xerox supervising the training of the workers.

As FIGHT found new sources of financial and technical support, it was able to function as its own bargaining agent. The friends looked for and discovered new ways of becoming involved in the issues of the sixties. When the twin-track coalition dissolved after about two years, the Friends restructured into an "umbrella" coalition, called MetroAct, directed at improving the quality of urban life in Rochester. Other Friends became active in Monroe County politics, and won control of the county government for the Democrats in 1973.

In summary, FIGHT and Friends of FIGHT, the twin-track coalition between a militant black organization and white middle-class supporters, had common goals, were structurally separated but visibly related, developed independent and joint strategies, and reversed the roles of leaders and followers within the coalition. As tensions increased internally, and as alternative sources of income emerged for the black organization, the coalition dissolved. Symbolically, it had reflected the values of independence, interdependence, and equality for the minority. Rochester was unique because the coalition occurred before Stokely Carmichael issued his ringing cry for "Black Power" in the summer of 1966.

Some of the new inner city groups chose to accept white support under new "rules" of separation, visibility and control by blacks, in exchange for a support role for whites in black power organizations.

Camden, New Jersey: The Black Peoples Unity Movement (BPUM) and The Friends of BPUM

Another twin-track coalition emerged in Camden, New Jersey shortly after the 1967 urban disorders. Structurally identical to the one in Rochester, the goals, likewise, of this parallel coalition were to increase the economic and political power of blacks in this city.

Concerned clergy and civil rights leaders once again played a major role in this situation of conflict and cooperation. Hoping to fill the existent power vacuum in the black community, they invited Rap Brown to address the minority community in Camden. Brown's theme that evening in the spring of 1967 was:

Don't talk about black power!
Organize! Organize! Organize!
Organize and achieve black power!

In response, a young black, Charles Sharp, brought together other young men from the community who had also heard Rap Brown, and they began to organize. By fall of 1967, a group called the "Black Believers in Knowledge" emerged. Shortly afterwards it changed its name to the Black People's Unity Movement (BPUM), to reflect more clearly its basic ideology of black unity and black power. Like its counterpart in Rochester, the underlying principles of BPUM included separation from whites, the right to self-determination, and control over decisions that affected their lives.

Initially the only resources they had were committed young black men and women determined to bring about changes in the Camden power structure. Soon BPUM found an outside source of support: suburban whites seeking understanding and involvement. With it, the organization expanded.

The event that catalyzed the formation of the twin-track coalition in Camden occurred on May 2, 1968. BPUM had been contracted to "tell it like it is" in the suburbs, and had been holding weekly seminars before white audiences of about 250 persons. At that time, the mood among many whites was one of fear, anxiety, guilt and confusion. The assassination of Martin Luther King, Jr. that spring had further exacerbated the crisis and the feelings of both blacks and whites. Another summer was approaching. The BPUM sessions were frank and brutal, according to the account of one white participant:

For BPUM it was really the first opportunity to tell white people the way things were...they worked this (white) group over...they shouted, "either the suburbs has to do something to help the cities out of its dilemma...or else it will be burned to the ground."

On the evening of the fourth session, BPUM did not appear as scheduled. Early that morning they had moved a black family out of dilapidated housing in an urban renewal area and into a downtown hotel. Sharp decided to confront City Hall with the demand for decent housing for the family at a public meeting scheduled for that night. He called for white participation and support. According to the same informant, Sharp told suburbanites "We're not coming out tonight. A crisis has happened, and if you want to have a real good seminar, come on down."

About twenty-five whites came to witness the confrontation of BPUM with City Hall. They heard the promise of housing, and many stayed on to see the promise go unfulfilled. Tension mounted. Demonstrations, marches and sit-ins took place throughout the week-end. When blacks were attacked and dispersed by the police, growing numbers of whites who had remained in contact throughout the tense week-end, decided to set up a support group.

The following night, the Friends of BPUM was organized to mobilize white support in the suburbs. Blacks who were present endorsed the alliance and the support of the Friends.

Operating without any stated or explicit "rules of the game" the coalition experienced intermittent periods of clashes and cooperation during its first year. According to the Reverend Sam Appel, the Friends' chairman, the first interactions between the blacks and their white allies were heated and emotional. Despite conflicts, the alliance continued. Resources were rapidly mobilized and transferred to the blacks by their white supporters. In the first twenty months of the twin-track coalition, the two hundred and fifty members collected and dispersed to BPUM over $25,000 without strings attached. In addition, at almost every meeting, according to Appel, "emergency funds" were raised on the spot, at the request of the BPUM leaders. The Friends turned over their mailing list to the BPUM, which used the talents and skills of the members to help develop and implement economic development plans.

Participation in the joint confrontations with City Hall and in non-violence workshops led to the arrest of some of the whites. Sam Appel, along with two other Friends, was arrested in July 1969 on the charge of "conspiracy to incite assaults upon the police force of the City of Camden and to obstruct justice and due administration of the law." The white leaders were indicted and released on bail. After a legal battle lasting three years, the charges were finally dismissed.

Although costly in terms of time, money and anxiety for those involved, these harassment tactics by City Hall increased the base of support among white suburbanites. Membership grew to over three hundred and fifty. Federal funds were obtained from the State Department of Community Affairs, through the joint efforts of Friends and Legal Services Lawyers. Said Appel:

> We went in to support their cause before Commissioner Ylvisaker and they got their first grant of $119,000. And don't think that wasn't effective! Here's some blacks--a so-called militant group--going up and asking for a great deal of money from the State with white suburbanites supporting them and saying, "Yes, they ought to get it"!

BPUM received further economic support, mobilized by the Friends, through the United Presbyterian "Self-Development of People" Fund-- $150,000 in 1971.

With such financial and technical support from private and public sources, BPUM achieved economic independence. It organized these enterprises: the BPUM Industries, Inc., a clothing factory; a retail outlet shop for African clothes, objects and literature/ the Black Developers, Inc., a construction company; and a day care center. All employees were recruited from the black community.

In addition to its economic successes, BPUM continued to fight for changes in Camden's urban renewal programs and procedures and in its educational system. As of 1972, it had an economic and political base in the city, controlling close to one million dollars in economic assets.

With this economic and political independence, BPUM's interaction with the Friends decreased. Some Friends continued to support BPUM with small pledges, by shopping at its stores, and by educating suburban whites.

Although internal conflicts had almost disrupted the twin-track coalition in its early days, the parallel alliance succeeded in transferring resources to the black community. Clearly this did not solve the problems of the inner city. Continuing strategies and black-white cooperation are still essential. This coalition dissolved. An office of the Camden Metropolitan Ministry was turned over to the Black People's Unity Movement. Appel, in 1970, assessed his model as follows:

> Much still has to be done to create a truly interdependent and just community. But the BPUM and Friends of BPUM believe an effective way has evolved to get at it together.

Boston: Boston United Fund and The Fund for Urban Negro Development (B.U.F./FUND)*

Once more, in another section of the Eastern part of the country, a twin-coalition emerged. A similar combination of events led to the formation of the Boston United Fund followed shortly by the white support group called the Fund for Urban Negro Development. It happened in 1968, in Boston.

Almost immediately after the 1967 urban disorder, and responding to an appeal by Stokely Carmichael in Boston, two young blacks, John Young and Charles Turner, set out to organize the community. John Young, a chemical engineer, was the chairman of CORE. Charles Turner, a Harvard student, was a member of the Commission on Church and Race of the Massachusetts Council of Churches. Both agreed with Carmichael's call for "black power." They sought a coalition of existing organizations in the black community and, through this, the development of black unity, as a way to deal with the problems of powerlessness and alienation.

---

*This section is based almost entirely on the unpublished manuscript of John Peter Fernandez, Harvard Honors Thesis (1969) entitled *Black Unity: An Analysis of Black-White Cooperation.* This is a valuable study inasmuch as it is the only one written and analyzed from a minority perspective.

In January 1968, they invited all black groups in Boston to meet and discuss the idea of forming a united front. Blacks were urged to come together to discuss their beliefs and goals in order to create unity and to establish common ground.

The meeting attracted representatives from a wide range of groups in the Roxbury-North Dorchester areas, from integrationists such as the NAACP to the Black Panthers. The keynote speaker, Leroy Boston, set forth the urgency of the principles of separatism and black power as the basis for organization. Said he:

We are organizing around one common denominator--our blackness. We have to organize to survive. We cannot win unless we stand together on crucial issues. We must restrict genocide of the black race and the only way to do this is through black power and black control of the community.

When Martin Luther King, Jr. was assassinated, the Black United Fund, as it came to be called, took off. His death catalyzed the joining together of the diverse groups into a functioning "umbrella" coalition. It described itself as follows:

The United Front is not a *program organization*. Rather, it provides a *means* for determining the priorities of action. The individual organizations in the community should be the means of carrying out the programs.

As plans evolved, the need for funds and other resources became increasingly evident. It was clear, also, that these had to be found outside the black community, which was almost totally devoid of economic power. The problem was solved, at least temporarily, when a recently organized white group, searching for a representative "black power" group to support, approached the Black United Fund.

The white group was called the Fund for Negro Urban Development (FUND). Also moved by the assassination of Dr. King, two well-known white businessmen, Ralph Hoagland and Sheldon Appel, had mobilized a group of other prominent white executives, legislators, professionals, academics, and clergymen to try a "radically new approach" to the racial crisis. This predominantly male group defined the problem as the fact that, "the black American had finally become totally embittered with four hundred years of America's systematic deprivation of

what America announces as its ideals of equality." The FUND was described, in a printed brochure as:
- A white response to black needs and hopes
- An act of faith in the power of black leaders to responsibly serve the best interests of their community
- An investment in progress and peace in Roxbury
- An example set by a group of white people who want to establish bonds of confidence and cooperation with the black community--and to encourage their friends and neighbors to do likewise.

Thus, the twin-track coalition emerged between the BUF, a black group, and FUND, a white group.

From the very beginning, the two tracks were independent and separate groups, with the whites assuming supportive and responsive positions, rather than leadership roles. At the request of BUF, funds were raised and transferred to the black community coalition. Financial support "without strings" was an integral part of the new approach within the twin-track coalition model. FUND recognized that black power leadership needed to manage its own affairs and to create and administer its own programs. In its brochure, called *The Central Proposition,* the white group maintained that, "FUND's revolution is that it supports the black community's determination to do for itself what others have failed to do or prevented it from doing."

FUND set high goals for itself: to raise $10,000,000 in donated funds and $90,000,000 in low-interest, long-term loans. Most of the ten million dollars was to come from private individuals; loans were to be raised from the endowments of various institutions such as churches, schools, universities, corporations, investment institutions and foundations. It received a non-profit tax status, and set up a skills bank for the BUF to draw upon.

Unlike the other twin-track coalitions, FUND deliberately chose a non-salient posture, even in selecting its name. This group of whites did not wish a visible alliance with its minority-power partner, nor did it see publicity for itself as beneficial to blacks.

Regardless of this, FUND did gain publicity which, at one point, had serious repercussions. The facts revealed that visibility was a cost for some whites and a payoff for others. FUND came to provide a certain kind of status in the liberal community.

A major incident arose when two Boston newspapers

published an unauthorized story about the black/white coalition and included the white membership list. The reaction within FUND was immediate. Some members were upset beacause their names had not been listed; others were upset because their names *had* been listed. Some withdrew, terminating their financial support. The leadership quickly responded with a letter to its membership, calling the publicity "totally unauthorized," and reiterating that FUND had not changed its basic anti-publicity philosophy. It maintained its desire to avoid the traditional white paternalistic posture toward the black community and the use of FUND by whites for "sense of glory and expiation."

Cooperation continued despite this occurrence. Several public breakfasts were held at which the black leaders spoke to predominantly white audiences. Heated exchanges sometimes took place. But, for the most part, Fernandez notes, whites were inhibited about asking the question that mostly preyed on their minds: how was the money that they contributed to the Boston United Fund being spent? Desiring independence of whites, BUF was reluctant to provide any data on its program in Roxbury. Fernandez states that:

> A general lack of information tended to increase the suspicions and misunderstandings on the part of both organizations and create a tense atmosphere under which the two organizations worked. The Front adopted an aloof, condescending attitude toward FUND. It was a "work-with-us-on-our-terms-or-forget-it" attitude.

Despite the tensions due to undefined "rules of the game" FUND continued to raise monies for the black group. In one year's time, over $300,000 was transferred to BUF. In addition, according to a FUND report, technical assistance was provided in over 100 specific cases.

As a new type of exchange between blacks and whites, the BUF-FUND coalition was fraught with strain. But it was important in that it was attempting to create a new model of cooperation. As Charles Turner maintained:

> The Front doesn't see the funds that the FUND organization has been raising as a charity donation; it doesn't see the relationship of one between beggar and a giver. It sees the relationship between two organizations with a commitment to

do a job.

Recent evidence suggests that the black track of this coalition became the United Way, while the white track dissolved. Some positive results had been accomplished. Monies and skills were transferred "without strings" to the black community. The principles of mutual independence and interracial cooperation were supported.

A very similar model, with similar strengths and limitations was also being tried in Baltimore, Maryland between the Black Panther Party and the Friends of the Panthers.

*Baltimore, Maryland: The Black Panther Party and The Friends of the Panthers**

Since the beginning of 1966, law enforcement officials throughout the country had shown increasing concern over the new black militant organization--the Black Panthers. Incidents between the Black Panthers and the police gained widespread publicity, especially the Oakland shootout in which Little Bobby Hutton was killed. Even wider coverage was gained when J. Edgar Hoover, director of the F.B.I., branded the Black Panther Party the "most dangerous group in the United States." Again, the assassination of Martin Luther King, Jr. proved a turning point toward radicalism. Eldridge Cleaver, then a prominent Panther leader said:

...the death of Martin Luther King...exhausted the myth that you could get what you wanted without fighting, that when the plantation foreman cracks the whip, you turn the other cheek...

The most famous (or infamous) clash of all occurred in Chicago when Fred Hampton and another Panther were killed under highly questionable circumstances. Evidence presented to a jury showed that 82 to 99 shots had been fired by the police while only one shot could be attributed to the Panthers.

Opposition to the policies of overkill by the police

―――――――

*The substance of this section is based on the unpublished articles, "Black Panther Defense Groups in the White Community: Two Case Studies," University of Maryland, 1970, by Fred L. Pincus.

reverberated in the white liberal and radical communities. Cleaver maintained that repression had strengthened the Party.

By late 1969 and throughout 1970, the Black Panther Party had become a rallying point for radical whites, and had forced many liberal whites to insist that--at the very least--Panthers and other radicals should be treated fairly in the courts.

The catalyzing incident in Baltimore was described by Pincus as follows:

For three days the police held an around-the-clock-stake-out at the Panther office for no apparent reason. The stake-out was carried out by uniformed policemen in marked cars, and was fully publicized in the newspapers and on the radio and television. Then, on December 3, the Baltimore Gas and Electric Company announced that it was shutting off the electricity and heat in the Panther office because they owed $642 in back bills. When the Panthers refused to let workmen in to shut off the utilities, the Gas and Electric Company proceeded to dig up the streets in front of the office in order to shut off the gas and electric lines.

Response from white radicals and liberals was immediate. Two separate alliances developed with the Black Panther Party, from these differing ideologically-based white groups. The radicals aligned themselves visibly, calling themselves the "Friends of the Panthers." The liberals organized a group called the "Baltimore Committee Against Political Repression." Even this name was perceived as being too radical. So, to portray a more "positive" image, it was renamed the "Baltimore Committee for Political Freedom."

In this twin-track coalition, as in others, the major resource needed by the minority-power group was money. The white liberals had money, but were less willing to take the risk of being visibly involved. Their organization included older whites and a few black ministers. Covertly, they tried to use their influence with the Governor and city officials to stop the repressive tactics of the police. The young white radical students were small in numbers and had little money, influence or prestige. They did have some organizational skills, a "radical network" and a high commitment to the elimination of police harassment of all radicals. They were anxious to participate in alliances with blacks.

The major strategies developed and implemented during

the short life-span of this coalition were fund-raising, educational forums, and direct action demonstrations, including picketing and leafleting. In addition, the Friends of the Panthers attended the liberal committee's meetings and collected monies. Unlike the Friends, the liberals refused to turn funds over directly to the Black Panthers. Their policy was to raise money, pay the overdue $642 gas and electric bill directly, and withdraw.

Strategies of the Friends to gain publicity and supporters included both education and direct action. They initiated an educational forum on the topic of Panther repression, followed by picketing at the Central Police Station.

This activity attracted over one hundred people, reportedly consisting predominantly of white radicals, with a sizeable minority of white liberals and a few blacks. A petition "deploring repression and murder of members of the Black Panther Party" both throughout the nation and in Baltimore was signed by most of those present. Funds were collected and committees organized. Picketing by whites in front of the police station followed, with no incidents. All of the money raised was turned over to the Black Panthers with "no strings."

Meetings continued on an irregular basis, with black leaders attending periodically. As in the other twin-tracks, lack of regularized interaction and clarity of the "rules of the game" strained the ties of the black and white partners. Lack of communication was a major weakness within this coalition. The conflict it created is well illustrated by the incident of the "Red Squad."

The Friends wrote and distributed a leaflet about the "Red squad" within the police department, without checking it out with the Panthers. The Panthers reacted strongly, furious about a particular statement in the leaflet which they felt should not have been included. The incident aggravated the relationships between the two tracks, even though the Friends admitted their tactical error in not consulting with the Panthers first. The reversed roles--blacks as leaders and whites as supporters--frustrated the young and active whites, many of whom found it "unusual" and "uncomfortable." The Friends of the Panthers had to come up with ideas which the Panthers either accepted or rejected. They criticized the black radicals for what they considered their lack of leadership.

This highlights an aspect of the twin-track coalition which appears to have presented problems in all of the cases examined: the reversed roles, which had not been adequately discussed or clarified. This was true even though white leadership agreed that whites working within the context of Panther support groups had to be willing to accept Panther leadership.

This twin-track coalition dissolved after about two and a half months, due both to the internal tensions described and changing external conditions. Overt police harassment of the Black Panthers began to abate and party membership shrank. The war in Vietnam accelerated, attracting both white radicals and liberals to the anti-war movement, a more fightable cause.

Although the coalition described was a temporary one, with many weaknesses, Fred Pincus, a major architect of FOP, maintains his position that white liberals and radicals are needed. Liberals have access to money and influence among higher public officials, and help mold public opinion. Through mass demonstrations and "putting their bodies on the line," radicals can mobilize people against political repression. In addition to their function of raising money, Pincus notes that the major part of political education in the white community must be done by whites.

SUMMARY

This essay has examined the social phenomenon of twin-track coalitions, a partnership model between blacks and whites which emerged in the mid- and late sixties in the black power movement. The efforts reported reflected the ideals of separation and independence for the minority along with the pragmatic realism of interdependence and the need for interracial cooperation. Some cases succeeded in bringing some economic and political power to the minority-power group; others did not. The twin-track coalition model is a non-traditional, non-paternalistic one, having weaknesses as well as strengths. The almost simultaneous development of several twin-track coalitions demonstrates that in times of crisis, it is possible to find new ways of cooperating across racial and class lines.

SOURCES

Alinsky, Saul, *Rules for Radicals,* New York: Vintage Books, 1971.
―――――――――――*Reveille for Radicals,* New York: Vintage Books, 1969.
Carter, Barbara, "The FIGHT Against Kokak," *The Reporter,* April 20, 1967, pp. 28-31.
De Gramont, Sanche, "Our Other Man in Algiers," *The New York Times Magazine,* November 1, 1971.
Fernandez, John Peter, *Black Unity: An Analysis of Black-White Cooperation,* Unpublished Honors Thesis, Department of Government, Harvard University, 1969.
Hamilton, Charles V., "The Nationalist vs. The Integrationist," *The New York Times Magazine,* October 1, 1972.
Hawryluk, Alexander, *Friends of FIGHT,* unpublished dissertation Cornell University, University Microfilms, #68-878, 1967.
Pincus, Fred, *Black Panther Defense Groups in the White Community: Two Case Studies,* University of Maryland, 1970, unpublished.
Sanders, Marion K., *The Professional Radical: Conversations with Saul Alinsky,* Evanston: Harper and Row, 1970.
Sethi, S. Prakash, *Business Corporations and the Black Man: An Analysis of Social Conflict,* Scranton, Pa.: Chandler Publishing Co., 1970.
Stearn, Gerald Emanuel, "Rapping with the Panthers in White Suburbia," *The New York Times Magazine,* March 8, 1970.

INTRODUCTION TO PART THREE

BONDS THAT INTEGRATE

Our third section considers integration in basic groups and institutions of the society. We present a selection of varied approaches to the issue rather than attempt a thorough analysis of every institutional area. From a sociological viewpoint, William Spinrad surveys professional sports, public accommodations, military organizations, housing and labor unions. He isolates elements that usually encourage integration, that deemphasize characteristics irrelevant to performance. His claim is that whether or not integration "works" is due not solely to individual prejudices or lack of them, but to the structure of specific situations.

The contribution of psychologist Janet Ward Schofield and sociologist Elaine Patricia McGivern is based on the first author's three year participant observation study of a desegregated middle school in the Northeast. The aspect of Schofield's research presented here is an analysis of a successful student organization--the "Team Z Student Council." It was intended to and did foster a positive shared group identity among black and white seventh grade students. Sensitive teachers helped to structure a more relaxed and democratic atmosphere than students usually enjoy, but were there when needed. The authors explain what made this experiment work -- a case which appears to illustrate Spinrad's hypothesis.

Finally, Charles Willie's selection is written in an autobiographical style, informed by both a sociological and religious perspective. Here the personal and spiritual bonds of one marriage stand against group hostility and a racially separatist mood. There is confrontation and ultimately group reconciliation. This essay serves as a fitting prelude to the final section of the book, which throws a spotlight on personal bonds in and of themselves.

7

WHEN INTEGRATION WORKS

By

William Spinrad

My objective is to analyze, with reference to specific areas of American life, when and why integration seems to "work", to be termed relatively "successful". For the account to be complete, some attention has to be given to the other side, some explanation presented of why there has not been more integration in these fields and related ones. The particular areas chosen are illustrative, rather than comprehensive or necessarily the most important. I touch upon: professional sports, public accommodations, military organizations, labor unions, and housing.

WHAT IS INTEGRATION?

My application of the term integration is based upon its meaning when it is made an issue, what those who call for integration actually intend. Initially, it is simply the opposite of forced segregation, of the deliberate prevention of black entry into something that is considered a special white domain. It also implies a kind of "togetherness" of equals in some common effort or experience. An operating definition of integration that "works", or is "successful", involves the idea that a significant number of people see it as an ongoing, acceptable, proper way of living or functioning. Additionally, successful integration is not a temporary, ephemeral situation, but continues to exist, even though it would be extremely difficult to stipulate a precise duration.

This does not assume there is no preference for being with

one's own, no ethnic identities, no conflicts between groups. A useful analogy illustrates the point. The major religious groups--Catholic, Jewish, and the various Protestant denominations and the non-minority ethnics--Irish, Italian, German, and others are generally "integrated" into American society. This does not eliminate "clannishness" or fights over whose ideals are better or who gets a bigger share of power and rewards. But, typically, none are pushed aside--segregated. The context of overall integration can limit such conflicts to realistic issues rather than perpetually festering sores. The issues can be resolved in a definite, if frequently temporary, decision which all sides accept.

Look at the example of religious groups. In past American history, particularly in the earliest colonial settlement, religious denominations were very separate from each other, and sometimes involved clearcut discriminations. In general, this is much less true today. Yet, consider -- the major religious groupings, Protestants, Catholics, and Jews, have fought over such questions as prohibition, gambling, divorce, birth control, abortion...

GENERAL ATTITUDES AND THEIR SIGNIFICANCE

Many people, with varying degrees of sophistication, have insisted that racial integration depends on changing, in some way, what "is in people's hearts"--the attitudes members of an ethnic group hold toward members of other groups. Most of the literature on the subject implies that it is predominately a "white problem", the search for ways of eliminating, or at least reducing, white prejudices towards blacks. Such an orientation tends to play down the relevance of black attitudes, to deny blacks an autonomous role. Nevertheless, because of this emphasis in research and discussion, I shall also have to concentrate, although not exclusively, on white attitudes.

Without discounting the value of efforts to improve general attitudes on racial questions, it is one of my major contentions that workable and successful integration depends more on feelings about *concrete situations*. Furthermore, just as prejudiced attitudes are often the result of actual practices rather than the cause, so do changes in attitudes frequently follow changes in practices and policies, as shall be seen. If one dwells only on general, abstract opinions as indicated by polling studies, white acceptance of the *idea* of integration has steadily increased, with occasional ups and downs.

In some cases, such changes parallel actual increases in the amount of integration, as in work situations and public accommodations. In others, however, such as the vital areas of housing and schools, segregation (or the rejection of integration) is just as evident as ever. Interestingly, many integrated housing developments functioned when white attitudes were less favorable to the idea, and when official policy was, at best, less sympathetic. Successful integration is thus more than a matter of general attitudes. In fact, as will be shown, general attitudes may sometimes be of minor significance.

THE CONDITIONS FOR SUCCESSFUL INTEGRATION

The meaning of integration, as well as the reasons for successful integration, may well be suggested by what has happened in professional sports. While agreeing in advance that it took a long time in coming, that continuing racist practices have been documented, that the entire idea can be oversentimentalized and covers an essentially peripheral aspect of American life, sports do present one of the most integrated areas of our society. The explanation was, perhaps, fittingly symbolized by an event that occurred in the National Basketball Association's 1975 championship playoff game between the Golden State Warriors and the Capital Bullets, both, interestingly, with black coaches, Al Attles and K. C. Jones.

In the final game, won by the Warriors, a Bullet player, Mike Riordan, climbed all over Rick Barry, the star of the Warriors, with the apparent objective of provoking a fight and getting them both tossed out of the game. Both players are white. The furious Attles immediately went after Riordan. Even though restrained by his players, he was ejected by the officials. Whether this prompted more vigorous playing by his team to ultimate victory is, of course, wild conjecture. What is important for our purpose is that the race of the participants was completely irrelevant. The melee that occurred would probably have been the same regardless.

Each team was integrated around a common purpose, to win--with all the appropriate rewards for professional athletes. They all had the same position as players, even if some, whatever their race, were more spectacular and prominent than others. The experience was generally satisfying for most players throughout the season; even "losers" did fairly well. Finally, the surrounding climate of opinion, the expectations of players and fans, as well as the demands of the organizations in which they worked, emphasized that all had to be in it together. Whether any players had racial prejudices, how friendly they were off the court, is unknown and, for this purpose, unimportant. To perform in that situation they had to accept integration. It is likely, furthermore, that any prejudices which might impede success were diminished (even if not completely eliminated) in the process.

This, then, is what integration is all about. The essential formula is that, whatever the amount and type of prejudice or lack of prejudice, people will accept or reject integration because of the requirements of specific *situations.* Here we have the other side of the notion of "institutional racism" --a situation which is structured to deemphasize characteristics irrelevant to performance. The elements that encourage integration, as suggested in the basketball account, can be outlined as follows:

1. common effort or experience, with which both blacks and whites identify.
2. equal status for both
3. satisfactions, or at least absence of dissatisfactions, in the total situation, not directly related to the fact of racial contacts itself.
4. a climate of opinion favorable to integration, resulting from the official, clearly communicated, position of those in power.

This formula also helps to explain why some attempts at integration do not "work," or why those which are immediately "successful" do not always continue that way. One or more of these conditions do not hold. An additional proposition flows from this scheme. Although the interracial attitudes of many people may become generally more favorable as a result of experience in integrated situations, those of others remain very "situational". This is, they do not necessarily accept integration in other types of situations.

The potential usefulness of these formulations will be examined now by applying them to other specific integration attempts: the widely divergent areas of public accommodations, military organizations and labor unions. A more extensive probing of the crucial subject of housing follows.

PUBLIC ACCOMMODATIONS

Integration of public facilities in the South, following the passage of the 1964 Federal Civil Rights Law, is widely accepted by now. In retrospect, it may seem like a small achievement, merely making the South similar to the North in this regard. That is probably why so little attention is paid to the subject with few comprehensive reports available on what has actually happened. For instance, the voluminous 1971 Report of the U.S. Civil Rights Commission, which goes into great detail on the enforcement of other Federal civil rights policies, devotes only a few paragraphs to public accommodations. Yet, one cannot forget how important all this once was-the presumed tenacity of Southern adherence to Jim Crow practices, the Montgomery bus boycott, the sit-ins at lunch counters that started the protest actions, and the image of Lester Maddox standing with his axe handle in front of his chicken emporium.

Although there is little concrete information about developments within the last fifteen years one may assume that, in general, this objective of the 1964 law has been achieved. The U.S. Commission's Report simply announces that "thousands" of facilities have complied, adds that there are still a "substantial" number of complaints, but specifies only two; these two involved bus terminal facilities in Greenville and Jackson, Mississippi. It is possible that such integration works because the four elements are present. The official position is strongly in favor of it. Black and white customers and guests share the same status in a common experience. The food and ambiance remain the same when someone from another race is present.

MILITARY

It is very ironic that military organizations, by their nature the most caste-like and the most thoroughly segregated federal government institutions for a long time, have become one of the most integrated features of American life. Formerly, the military leadership accepted segregation in the armed forces as a reflection of the national scheme. Pressures for integration became meaningful with the growth of a mass military force in World War II, with its ideological emphasis on the totalitarian enemies and the racism of the principal adversary. The official response was along the lines of avoiding trouble-the idea that the military is dedicated to effective operation, not "social experimentation". Nevertheless, some investigations of servicemen's attitudes revealed that, here too, integration might "work". One specific finding was particularly significant. When white soldiers were asked about their willingness to serve in integrated units, those with the closest previous military contact with blacks were most likely to accept the principle.

The process of integrating the armed forces was slow but steady. The sometimes reluctant decision of military officialdom to take the next step was facilitated, throughout, by continuing investigations of servicemen's attitudes. Later results were similar to those of the World War II studies, including findings under combat conditions in Korea. In Vietnam, integration occurred down to the smallest organized unit, the squad, in the army, and both white and black non-commissioned officers.

For most of the services, largely conscripted until recently, one can hardly define their experiences as typically "pleasant", especially in war time. The four requirements I suggest were present. What whites and blacks shared in the services is the same status in a common set of activities. They are all, in the old military jargon, simply "GI's" in a common context. The official policy is now openly pro-integration. Many factors affect the various concrete situations in which they are involved, in training or in combat, but the presence of members of another race does not make it any better or worse.

Again, the specific situational consequences must be considered. Racial incidents have indeed occurred, some well-publicized. Few of these seem to involve features exclusive to military life. They usually take place in leisure activities or away from the base or field unit. Acceptance of integration, and the diminishing of hostile attitudes, may not always extend to these areas of a serviceman's life. In general, integration in purely "social" situations in the military seems the most difficult. Note too that "integration" is obviously limited in the higher levels of the military hierarchies.

UNIONS

The media, and some black spokesmen, have depicted labor unions as among the most segregated institutions in society and thus particularly inimical to blacks' needs and aspirations. Without getting into this complex controversial question in any detail, the important central area that must be emphasized is that such accusations are directed primarily not at "industrial" unions, but at "craft" unions, or craft aspects of industrial unions. Craft unions generally cover skilled workers in smaller work settings, where the union has some control over entry into the job. Industrial unions comprise a variety of workers, mostly, but not exclusively, semi-skilled, in large industrial enterprises, and the union has no impact on entry into the job--in fact has little interest in such a vast responsibility. In the craft situations, aspiring blacks may be seen as rivals for highly-desirable positions believed to be scarce. Hostility may be partially based upon the fact that they are black, but it is readily extended to other groups. In fact, entry to the skilled trades is frequently reputed to be historically reserved for relatives and friends.

In industrial unions, white and black workers typically do the same type of job, and often develop a sense of solidarity around the common activity, based upon generally equal status in building and maintaining the unions. Even the entry of blacks to the jobs is supported by whites, because of the fear that otherwise blacks will be used against them. The history of the use of blacks against whites, and vice versa, in industrial relations was clearly appreciated by the organizers of industrial unions. As one of them explained, "we learned years ago through bitter experience that we cannot afford to have any disruption or break in our Negro-White relations among workers. They are all workers faced with common problems for which the union fights and on which we have to stay together." When this idea is forcefully communicated to the membership, and is further supported by government anti-discrimination doctrines, it establishes a climate of opinion which can help sway prejudiced white workers to become proponents of Fair Employment Practices, as, for example, among "white ethnic" auto workers in Detroit and ones from Southern rural backgrounds. Accordingly, they have also frequently voted for black workers in positions of shop and local leadership. As a further indication of how an industrial union can foster interracial solidarity, a study of one specific local showed that the white workers most likely to accept blacks as work colleagues tended to be those most involved in union activities, and all of them were not necessarily "unprejudiced" or in favor of integration in other areas of their lives. This helps explain why, whatever the justifiable criticism that can be made of unions on racial grounds, blacks have obtained more responsible leadership positions in them than in any other type of American institution.

In employment integration, the impact may also be very situational. Some of the same white workers who show strong feelings of job and union solidarity with blacks may be very hostile to the idea of blacks moving into their neighborhoods. They even join in activities to prevent that possibility. Many "good union" auto workers were active in trying to forestall school busing in the Detroit area.

Integration in industrial unions does not mean that internal conflicts are never related to racial alignments, just as has been true of other ethnic affiliations. In fact, integration may facilitate continuing realistic conflicts. Within the accepted union solidarity various people may want more of something, including the better jobs and union offices. This is often associated with other features, such as length of time on the job and in the union. Integration does not mean perpetual peace and harmony. In fact, organized black caucuses appear most frequently in industrial unions. However, conflicts may be racial only by historical coincidence, as exemplified by controversy over seniority rights. Since black workers have typically not been on the job or in the factory as long as many white workers, some view seniority rules in relation to layoffs and promotions as discriminatory. However, senior black workers in such industries as auto and steel are also defensive about seniority rights.

Since black workers will tend to be the last hired, the fear of also being the first fired could produce a severe type of internal union conflict, eliciting a racial confrontation in time of recession. In many cases, the solidarity within many unions (of which integration is essentially, a by-product) has prompted various attempts to find alternative ways of meeting the problems of layoffs, and thus ease the potential of racial clashes. Some examples include: sharing short work weeks, rotating layoffs, dismissing first those high seniority workers who can enjoy sufficient unemployment benefits. Race is obviously not the only feature involved, but such approaches do, in the actual existent situation, symbolize the socially-and racially-integrated character of industrial unions.

THE COMPLEX PROBLEM OF INTEGRATED HOUSING

Creating and maintaining integrated residential patterns remains a crucial and most thorny problem, of which school segregation is a direct by-product. In this case, attitudes towards integration among whites have become much more favorable than the actual amount of integration. On the basis of a complicated series of measures, desegregation did increase slightly from 1960 to 1970. For instance, one 1968 study of whites in fifteen large cities found that 62% agreed that "Negroes have a right to live anywhere they wish." However, the use of a more thorough list of questions in 1965 Gallup national survey, indicated that attitudes were more complex. Only 13% would move if a "Negro lived next door", but 40% would move if there were "large numbers of Negroes in the neighborhood". In other words, abstract acceptance of the idea of residential integration does not necessarily reflect actual reactions to integration in a personal situation.

Nevertheless, integrated developments and residence have existed, some for a considerable amount of time. Understanding why those have succeeded to some extent may also supply clues as to why there are not more examples, given the general decrease of racial prejudice. To start with, some neighborhoods became integrated by historical accident, lost in the record, and have remained so because of general neighborhood stability--few and slow changes in people or in buildings or use of buildings.

Particularly interesting are the experiences in public housing, especially low-cost housing projects, which provided the most complete studies of the effects of integration back in the later 1940's and early 1950's, when white attitudes were less favorable and official national policy was less heavily weighted towards integration. One well-publicized research project described in the book *Interracial Housing*, by Morton Deutsch and Mary Collins, utilized what amounted to a laboratory situation-- integrated and de facto segregated projects in neighboring cities. Although public housing in Newark, New Jersey was officially integrated, black and white residents lived in different buildings, frequently separated by streets. The projects studied in New York City were completely integrated. A sample of housewives in two projects in each city, each development containing from 40% to 70% black tenants, was interviewed

The results were very striking. Personal relations between members of the two races were much more conspicuous in the integrated projects, extending, for many, to frequent mutual home visits and going out together. Similarly, integrated tenants were, on a variety of measures, much more likely to have favorable attitudes towards members of the other race. Most pertinently, a sizeable majority of whites in the integrated settings reported development of more favorable attitudes over time, while about two-thirds in the segregated pattern indicated no change.

In this situation, integration not only "worked" but resulted in better relations and better feelings between the two groups, although, obviously, all were not similarly affected. Accordingly, about two-thirds of white women in the integrated projects liked living in such a setting, and over half preferred it as a general housing policy. In contrast, only 5% of those in the building-segregated settings favored housing integration as a policy. In essence, this explains one reason for the apparent success for the New York experience in the projects studies. The women in the integrated projects were responding to the existent official practice, indicated by a conspicuous tendency to believe that the management favored interracial friendships. This was not true of those in the segregated projects. Similarly, among those in the integrated project who had an opinion on the subject, the majority felt that their husbands and friends would look favorably on their interracial friendships, or at most, be neutral. This, too, was not typical in the Newark sample.

Other features of the situation facilitated successful integration. All had exactly the same status as tenants. At that time, getting into a low-cost public housing development was considered very worthwhile, not only because it provided an adequate residence at a reasonable cost, but because any housing was very desirable in the post World War II shortage. Most tenants were pleased with the facilities and services. The turnover rate was very low. The stigma more recently associated with low-cost public housing, developing out of fears about welfare families, crime, or vandalism were not evident, although there was some concern about conditions in nearby slums. In addition, the sense of a common experience and identity was intensified by widespread friendliness, a variety of tenant organizations and collective activities.*

The situational factor of living in an officially integrated setting with many interracial contacts, and participating in common experiences with equals, induced acceptance of the idea of residential integration, increased interracial associations, and produced more favorable interracial attitudes. To what extent was the impact also situational and to what extent was it more general? One significant finding has already been presented. About two-thirds liked their personal experience in an integrated project, but only about half thought this was a good policy. Over half of the whites said they had "respect for Negroes in the project", but fewer extended this to "Negroes in general". In other words, some of the white residents developed more inclusive improved interracial attitudes, but, others confined their acceptance of integration and of blacks as associates to the specific setting.

A follow-up study a few years later, in four projects in four unnamed "Eastern" cities, was more complicated.* Both low and middle income developments were included. Half were considered "building integrated" and half "building segregated", but the proportion of black residents was about 10% in each. Because

---

*Following the publication of the study, the Newark Housing Authority announced that the buildings in its projects would be integrated.

the number of blacks was so small, some white residents would live "near" blacks, and some "far", and the comparison between these two groups in both types of residence provided the primary analysis. As predicted, the "nears" generally had more personal contacts with blacks, more pleasant experiences with them, more favorable attitudes at the time and more reported changes in a favorable direction since they moved in. Interestingly, the women were asked about the subjects of conversations when whites and blacks became friendly, and the favorite topics were: schools, children, prices, and the project — logical and appropriate for everyone in that setting.*

There were several differences among the projects on these "near"-"far" comparisons, which were rather complex and unnecessary to explain for this account. The experiences of the "nears" generally made them more likely to believe that their white friends would approve their friendliness with blacks, made them feel that living in an integrated setting was worthwhile, and stimulated support for an integrated housing policy.

One aspect of this report must be clarified. Many of the whites in the building-segregated projects actually lived closer to blacks than many in the building-integrated projects, for some of the buildings actually had no blacks. This helps account for an important finding unexpected by the researchers. More white women in the "integrated" project supported the idea of residential segregation than was true in the "segregated" project, but, as indicated, a large number of the former were not experiencing genuine integration. The "near"-"far" comparisons are therefore more important. Furthermore, the authors pointed out some other important features that affected tenants' perception of the extent of integration. The official policies in the cities with building-segregated projects had been more clearly and consistently in favor of at least "project integration". Furthermore, the only integrated working staff, and integrated community and tenant organizations were in the building-segregated developments. Unlike the New York situation in the

---

*Daniel M. Wilner, Rosabelle Price Walkley, Stuart W. Cook, *Human Relations in Interracial Housing: A Study of the Contact Hypothesis,* Minneapolis, University of Minnesota Press, 1955.

earlier study, the climate in the "integrated" setting was thus not as definitively pro-integration.

The writer is unaware of any comparable studies since then. Relying on less careful or systematic accounts and reports, many other examples of integrated housing are on the record. If low-cost public housing now seems, for many, a kind of desperate last resort, this is hardly the case for middle-income housing. This is particularly true in a city like New York, where it is one of the best ways of obtaining a satisfactory residence at a reasonable price. From the information available, it appears that the turnover rate is generally not too high and replacements are waiting-- presenting the picture of a stable community, with, usually, good services and facilities in or nearby. Furthermore, residents often consider them very genuine communities because of the high degree of friendly informal contacts and the many organized activities.

All this is even more true of large cooperative developments, many of which are clearly racially integrated, sometimes through special efforts to attract black residents. (I am referring to authentic cooperatives, not the pseudo-luxury type where the coop is merely a device for claiming income deductions). It must be pointed out that coops, many of which are set up by groups such as unions and religious organizations, may attract the type of people most disposed towards integration in the first place. However, their histories also indicate two of the major problems affecting the possibilities of an integrated development remaining integrated. One is the very sensitive and not too well understood idea of the "tipping point", the notion that, when the proportion of blacks begins to get beyond a certain quantity, usually thought to be about one-third, the development will slowly, but irretrievably, become a segregated black project. In general, one can only surmise that sometimes this happens and sometimes it doesn't, but cooperative leaders, among both tenants and management, frequently make an early effort to maintain integration, generally avoiding the iniquitous idea of quotas. They strive to attract people of either race, depending on the concrete situation, in order to maintain something resembling an integrated situation.

The other problem involves the question of the deterioration of surrounding neighborhoods, which begin to pose typical fears about slum conditions, from anxiety about crime to concern about decline in services and facilities, including schools. One reported example is the large Rochdale cooperative in Queens, where the harmonious relations between black and white inside does not prevent widespread dismay about the surrounding area of poor blacks. As a result, there has been some exodus of residents, both white and black, but apparently more prominently white, with the future of this integrated coop therefore in doubt. This further suggests a very important and controversial theme that I have not explicitly mentioned until now-that questions of racial integration in contemporary America are usually associated with the issue of class difference.

The story of integration in more conventional private housing settings covers at least two distinctive types-those that become integrated by "natural" migration and the consciously-planned integrated communities. When the class feature is not prominent within the neighborhood itself, the problem may be more one of maintaining integration that its initial establishment--although this may also be difficult sometimes in the "natural" type, where "scare" selling and mass exodus occur. Yet, the difficulties and promises in both types are somewhat similar, so that my discussion will mainly emphasize the planned situations, which provide a better focus and for which there is more material.

The people who move into such planned developments, generally home owners, may be ones who are more inclined to accept integration beforehand. In most situations, however, this does not seem to be a primary motivation. People move there, and often stay there because they have good homes, frequently at a reasonable cost, in a pleasant environment with satisfactory services and facilities. The more successful ones are usually situated in somewhat isolated areas, where the impact of any possibly unpleasant neighborhood features are minimal.

As in the case of the public housing studies, an important reason for success is that the climate of opinion supports integration. In the planned communities this includes the developers and the sponsoring agencies. If nothing else, the white residents, as described by one realtor, "find out the world doesn't come to an end. People begin to say 'what's so bad about that'?" Of course, this implies that things are not "bad", that they have a decent house which is not too costly (and that one has actually been built), that they have proper facilities and services, that the surrounding area is not too unpleasant, which covers not only slum conditions but such structures as factories and railroad tracks.

When these conditions do not apply, both blacks and whites who want and can afford a decent home either fail to move in or leave; for well-known reasons, blacks have less choice. It either never becomes integrated or soon loses that character, in many cases later becoming a lower economic class area, typically largely black.

According to many experts, major social institutions, public and private, not only fail to project an official climate of opinion in favor of integration but are, at best lukewarm, and sometimes actively hostile. While laws and government administrative policies officially favor integration, the actual governmental personnel may not be avid in enforcing those regulations and, above all, the machinery for enforcement is (according to the U.S. Civil Rights Commission) usually inadequately staffed and financed. Therefore, officials do not sufficiently control the practices of their own people, nor those of private real estate firms, brokers and builders. This, according to many who are closest to the subject, is a greater obstacle to residential integration than any inherent interracial hostilities between black and white.

Some experts go further. They insist that government and private institutions frequently make special efforts to see that services are inferior in prospective or existing integrated settings. This, and the fear of what may happen to their neighborhoods, which they frequently regard as genuine communities, is what prompts so many whites to leave when integration is "natural", when many blacks simply move into the area, often encouraged by "blockbusting" realtors. To give one almost quaint example from an account of a district in Detroit: policial "Liberals", most in favor of integration in the abstract, were among the first to leave when blacks began to move into a white community, because they were concerned about what might happen to their schools. And, because of the comparative lack of political clout by blacks, educational, as well as other public facilities, do frequently decline under such conditions.

Class factors, as has been emphasized, complicate many

hoped-for trends towards more residential integration. My analysis thus far covers both white and black people who can be described as stable working class or middle class-white collar workers, professionals, or small business persons. (The question of integration for the few very high status and affluent blacks is a different issue, outside our immediate concern). Integration with the large number of "underclass" blacks, usually identified as the "poor", is much more problematical. The reluctance of whites to live near poor whites is probably still present, but not very meaningful. Poor blacks, and those from other minorities, are more forcefully resisted as neighbors, particularly if they come in significant numbers. While racial prejudice may be involved, it is at least related to something seeming to be much more immediately real. Whatever the reasons, people simply fear the possible decline in services and facilities, the purported loss in property values, the spread of serious social problems, and possible disappearance of the neighborhood and the community they know.

Some of these sentiments are difficult to eradicate and may represent nothing but vague forebodings, similar to the motivation of those who oppose such things as half-way houses for former mental patients near their homes. But some of these anxieties may be eased by dispersing the residences of the poor, especially the black poor. In this way, services and facilities could be at the proper level and problems limited. Both class and racial integration would then be possible. This is the hope behind the advocates of scatter-site low cost public housing, despite the turmoil that the idea has provoked in various places. This is a principal motive behind those who are combatting zoning restrictions which prevent the poor from living in many suburbs. One very ambitious attempt at such integration is officially under way in the Miami County area around Dayton, Ohio. Each community has been given its "quota" of low cost housing, more to the wealthier ones, and no development is to be near any existent ghetto. This little-publicized breakthrough should be closely watched, particularly by those interested in a racially-harmonious society.

CONCLUSION

Naturally, only a few aspects of American society can be considered in this brief paper. The most obvious omission is any discussion of the complicated, perplexing problems encompassing efforts to obtain school integration in the absence of more residential integration, which would probably require another complete article. In different ways, the analysis of such widely-divergent subjects as professional sports, public accommodations, military organizations, unions, and housing developments should provide useful clues for appreciating some of the reasons for successful integration or its absence.

Prior interracial attitudes and contacts may have a bearing for some, but the concrete experience is all important for most. Pertinent elements have been spelled out for consideration for each of the situations considered. Recognition of a common effort or experience among equals is paramount. Intensive identification with that experience, as exemplified by the "good unionist" in an industrial union and the actively-involved tenant in an integrated project, increases the likelihood of accepting integration. The experience should be generally satisfying, above and beyond the existence of integration, as best illustrated by the various integrated-housing efforts. The perceived climate of opinion nurtured by both official sources and peers, should be clearly favorable to integration. The conclusion that must be added is that, for many who learn to accept integration, their acceptance will not necessarily extend to other situations where the favorable previously described conditions are not present.

8

CREATING INTERRACIAL BONDS IN A DESEGREGATED SCHOOL*

By

Janet Ward Schofield and

Elaine Patricia McGivern

This paper describes and analyzes the development of a positive group identity shared by black and white students in a desegregated school. This exploration is useful because such shared identities are not the automatic result of formal desegregation. This fact is captured with vivid simplicity by a student in a desegregated high school who told researchers George Noblit and Thomas Collins: "All the segregation in the city was put (here) in one building." Indeed, a wide variety of studies, make it clear that a high degree of racial isolation is common in desegregated schools. This is unfortunate, as both theory and research demonstrate that racial isolation has numerous negative consequences.

Creating a sense of shared identity in desegregated schools is a particularly important process since people often respond to each other, at least initially, primarily as blacks or whites rather than as individuals who are, among other things, black or white. Given the history of race relations in this country and the contemporary socio-economic disparities between the races, it is not surprising that children frequently attach quite negative evaluations to racial outgroups. This, of course, makes continued racial isolation with its attendant negative consequences more likely. And such separation, in turn, may lead to the confirmation of stereotypes.

Even if children did not bring learned negative evaluations into play when dealing with others labelled as white or black, research suggests that just perceiving oneself as a member of one group and perceiving another as a member of a different group can lead to insidious comparisons. Tajfel and his associates investigated the effects of dividing individuals into groups and supplying labels which allow them to categorize others as "in-group" or "out-group" members. Typically, in these experiments the basis for group membership is some relatively unimportant characteristic designed to form a weak basis of group membership. Even so, discrimination against out-group members is a consistent result. In-group members are typically rated more favorably than out-group members, according to Doise and his associates.

What are the implications of the preceding for structuring desegregated schools? One idea which comes to mind immediately is that race as a social category should be ignored or minimized in every possible way in such schools. This tactic, however, contains numerous pitfalls. First, it runs counter to the value and importance of fostering positive group identity, a recent emphasis by blacks and other American ethnic groups. Secondly, there is some evidence that even if this were desirable, it is unlikely to work. The senior author found that in a school in which the staff adopted what Rist has called a "colorblind" perspective and placed a virtual taboo on the discussion of race, children's perceptions of and reactions to each other were still heavily influenced by racial group membership.

An alternate approach to handling the potentially negative impact on intergroup relations of children's use of race as a category for perceiving themselves and others is to consider creating new, supplemental group identities which cut across racial boundaries. Instead of engaging in the undesirable and probably futile strategy of trying to obliterate group identity, one could try to create meaningful additional membership in interracial groups. To the extent that this is achieved, black and white children will then become "in-group" members for each other, at least in contexts which make this group membership relevant. This paper describes and analyzes the development of one such in-group, a student council for seventh grade students.

The data on which the paper is based come from a three-year study of the development of social relations among students in a desegregated school. The basic methodology, described more fully elsewhere, was the observation of students' behavior in a wide variety of formal and informal school setting. We employed the "full field notes" method of data collection for non-participant observation.

THE WEXLER MIDDLE SCHOOL

Wexler Middle School serves 1600 students in grades six through eight and is located in a large northeastern industrial city*. The school opened in 1975 under an "open enrollment policy". Students were selected on a first-come, first-serve basis within predetermined race and sex quotas set to ensure a student body which was roughly fifty percent black.

The seventh grade students who are the focus of this report entered the school as sixth graders in 1975. While most white students typically came from middle or upper-middle class neighborhoods, black students tended to come from working class neighborhoods. A large majority of the students who entered Wexler in 1975 had previously attended *de facto* segregated elementary schools.

The school's unusual efforts to provide an ideal environment for interracial education can be illustrated by its staffing pattern. The top four administrative posts are evenly divided between blacks and whites. Similary, each grade has two counselors, one black and one white. About 25 percent of the faculty are black.

Commitment to fostering positive intergroup relations is also shown in the school's support of an extensive array of activities specifically designed to help students to get to know one another. One such program was the Directed Activity (DA) program. The DA's were club-like activities held twice a week during the school day. So, for example, there were DA's devoted to listening to records, producing a play, and building model cars and airplanes. The seventh grade "student council" discussed in this paper was one of the DA activities.

* To protect anonymity, pseudonyms are used for all names, including that of the school, mentioned in this paper.

THE TEAM Z STUDENT COUNCIL

The idea for the establishment of a student council as a directed activity came from Ms. Baker, a teacher on Team Z. (At Wexler, the word team is used to describe a group of approximately 150 children who all have the same academic teachers. Each team is divided into five classes which rotate among the team's teachers.) The impetus for setting up the student council flowed from Ms. Baker's belief that teachers have a very real responsibility to try to foster positive relations between black and white students. This belief is expressed in her comment to a field observer,

I think you have to foster positive relations through the teacher... You can't throw students together and say they're going to come out loving each other. That's not going to happen if they're thrown together... Let them feel safe and secure, (then) race relations will be improved; but it comes from teachers and administrators.

Ms. Baker felt that one way of improving relations between black and white children was to create a shared sense of belonging to a group.

The problem here is the kids don't feel like they actually belong. I am thinking of setting up a student council for this team... I think the team is the place to start... When I asked students about this and told them that I would be having a student council, directed activity, so many of the students wanted to sign up, that I had to discourage them. I had about 80 that wanted to sign up...

The student council, which began in December 1976, lasted until June 1977. The council, which retained the same officers throughout its six-month existence, was composed of 11 black females, 5 black males, 9 white females and 8 white males. Meetings were held in the open classroom area of the language arts and social studies room on Wednesday afternoons. Two seventh grade teachers directed this activity. One was Ms. Baker, the black language arts teacher who initiated the idea. The other was Mr. Count, a white social studies teacher.

The student council planned many activities and undertook responsibility for their own organization. Among the social events they organized were Valentine's Day party, a roller-skating party, baseball team, a picnic, and a talent show. They also had a wide variety of fund-raising events, such as a raffle and a bake sale. What is important is not so much the particular activities chosen, but rather how these students went about organizing and carrying them out. The students achieved the goals they set for themselves. But more importantly, they developed a strong sense of group unity as a result. This sense of unity was promoted both by the actions of the teachers who took responsibility for the council and by the organizational structure they provided for carrying out routine council activities.

During the first meeting, Ms. Baker outlined the format the student council would follow by presenting three related yet distinct themes. She discussed changes in the traditional roles of teachers and students as council participants, indicated the behaviors she expected from both teachers and students which, at least implicitly, would vary from norms applicable to usual classroom behavior, and emphasized the team as an in-group. Ms. Baker opened the meeting by stating that the council was only for Team Z students. Other seventh grade students would not participate.

> We won't allow other kids to be in this. This is just for us. I am not going to act like a teacher. In two weeks I expect you to be on your own. All that I am going to do is to get you started and give you some guidance on the best ways to begin... Within two weeks I expect you to be able to discuss your own business, conduct your own meetings, set up your tables and chairs...the way you think they should be set up....

With these statements, Ms. Baker redefined the teacher's role as one of a resource person who provides guidance and offers suggestions rather than as one who teaches and disciplines. She placed responsibility for conducting the meetings with the students themselves. Some of the norms imposed in their academic classes were modified in the student council setting. For example, students could rearrange the furniture, sit wherever they wished and set the topics for discussion. By defining members of the student council as an in-group with special norms and roles, Ms. Baker provided a framework for the development of a sense of group identity that could cross-cut their important social identities, namely race and sex.

The emphasis given in this first meeting to the council as

a legitimate arena for the expression of conflicting opinions is also of significance.

Ms. Baker continued, "What is a council for? Raise your suggestions to each other...Mr. Count and I are here to support you. We'll have disagreements with each other. We'll even talk loudly. That's what goes on in Washington with Senators and Representatives.

Since the ground rules for disagreement were defined by analogy to Congress, students could understand that conflicts of opinion were not to be perceived as disruptive, nor to be disapproved. Thus, council could retain its unity in spite of the differences of opinion which would inevitably arise in setting priorities and planning activities.

As students began their discussion of the purpose of the council, the initial focus of their ideas was on very general themes such as "making Team Z the best" or "helping Team Z"; but soon they began to develop some themes which reflected specific shared concerns:

A black boy, Don, raises his hand. Pointing to another black boy, Stan, he says, "Stan has a good idea, but he's afraid to say it." Ms. Baker replies, "Don't be afraid. I'm not your teacher here." Stan says he thinks it would be a good idea to have hall monitors to take the names of the kids who litter the halls... Another child says, "And what about gypping in the cafeteria."

These suggestions for group discussion were greeted with enthusiasm. An especially high level of concern was expressed with regard to "gypping" which is the act of cutting into a line of students who are waiting for lunch in the school cafeteria. Nearly all of the students felt that "gypping" was a serious problem. Their first council decision was to nominate two temporary cafeteria line monitors, Bill and Jerry, both black males, who would begin their duties the next day. At the next meeting the council appointed hall monitors, two white girls, a black boy, and a white boy, and two permanent cafeteria monitors, both black boys.

Both black and white students also expressed concern over the extent of physical contact, such as the bumping, shoving, and "hasseling" that went on in the halls between classes, as well as occasional fights. Studies show that in desegregated schools, both black and white students often perceive blacks as at least somewhat more likely to be involved in this type of activity than whites. At Wexler, too, interviews suggest that black and white students share the perception that blacks and especially black boys, are more likely than whites to be involved in incidents of fighting and intimidation. This perception can lead to anxiety on the part of white students, as well as to their having generally negative reactions to black students.

The student council's actions had clear potential to diminish the extent to which such rowdy behavior would lead to strain in black-white relations. First, the discussion in the student council made it clear to all children that many blacks as well as whites wanted to enjoy more order in their environment, and to control aggressive or thoughtless behavior. Second, it was widely agreed that having hall and cafeteria monitors did cut down on the amount of disruptive behavior which occurred. Finally, Ms. Baker was not adverse to mobilizing peer pressure in the student council to get children to act in an orderly and friendly way in other school contexts.

Ms. Baker points out that Team Z children who are accused of an infraction of the rules will come up before the council. The council will adjudicate these disputes.

In February, the student council vice-president was taken before the council because of complaints which had been lodged against him.

Ms. Baker says, "Bill, I have heard reports that you are misbehaving, that you have been running in the halls... Some students have questioned whether... you should (continue) as vice-president... Perhaps we should have a vote in class to decide whether or not Bill should continue in his capacity as vice-president... If Bill...cannot...set a good example, maybe he should not be our vice-president any more..."

After discussing Bill's misconduct, council voted to place him on probation for two weeks, and to remove him from office if his behavior did not improve by the end of that time. In this illustration, the students applied sanctions for behavior that violated group norms, such as the often expressed idea that student council members should set an example for others. Thus the council helped not only to create a sense of group identity through positive, enjoyable activities, but also to control negative behaviors which were aversive to most children and potentially harmful to relations between blacks and whites.

Although Ms. Baker used peer pressure effectively to change negative behavior, she also tried to instill in the children a sense of concern for each other's feelings. Indeed, she even assigned students the responsibility of protecting other council members from the possibly unfeeling behavior of others. She utilized the idea of students protecting each other's feelings as a means of emphasizing the identity of the student council as a unified group. This theme occurred in Ms. Baker's remarks as early as the council's second meeting:

> Okay, you kids that are on the student council, when our kids make (election campaign) speeches to the whole team they'll be nervous. Don't let anyone laugh at them or giggle. I listened to the speeches and they are all excellent. You are doing a good job and I'm proud of you.

Some students picked up so readily on this theme that by February they felt free to challenge behavior not considered sufficiently respectful of other's feelings, even if it was initiated by the teacher herself. For example when Ms. Baker suggested that the student council should discuss their vice-president's conduct, the following occurred:

> Penny, a white girl, raised her hand. Ms. Baker said, "Yes, Penny?" Penny replied, "Ms. Baker, I think maybe you should talk to Bill privately so we don't embarrass him here in class." Ms. Baker responded, "Well, I've decided I'm going to do it now, but not in a way that will embarrass Bill."

The four student council officers, a president, vice-president, secretary, and treasurer, were elected early in the council's history. Analysis of the nominations for these offices and the conduct of the campaign suggest a number of points of interest. Nominations were held during the first meeting. Three white boys, four white girls, five black boys, and three black girls were nominated. About two-thirds of the time, ten times in all, children were nominated by others identical to them in both race and sex, indicating the importance of both of these factors in the social life of students at Wexler. There were, however, four cross-race nominations compared to only one cross-sex nomination. The black girl eventually elected as council president was nominated by a white girl.

Although the nominations showed a marked tendency to favor both racial and sexual in-groups, interracial campaign committees were very common. Perhaps one reason for this was that immediately after the nominations and before the creation of these committees, Ms. Baker presented this explicit ground rule, "In this campaign there will be no racial, ethnic, or religious themes. You will not vote for someone because of sex, race, or religion. Nor will kids be allowed to campaign on that basis." Field notes taken during the council's second meeting illustrate the biracial nature of the campaign committees as well as the fact that the committee structure was very conducive to cooperation.

Five boys, two black, three white, congregate at a rear table. One of them is Bill, a black, who is running for vice-president. As Bill sits down, John, a white, tousles Bill's hair. The other black at the table, Mark, has begun to write a speech for Bill. He pauses to ask if there are any campaign posters. Bill says "No." 'Well, I'll make some," replies Mark. He leaves and returns with construction paper, pencils and crayons. John has joined another group. The remaining four boys discuss slogans. It is a friendly and animated discussion as they offer slogans and then reject them. Eric, who is white, says, "I'll vote for you, Bill." Eric is running for treasurer. After additional concentrated discussion, the boys decide on a single slogan, "Vote for Bill, he's the best. He'll do better than all the rest." Each takes paper and starts working on a poster.

The campaign committees are only one example of the large number of committees which were formed to help students plan their various activities. Students generally volunteered for a committee without knowing who else would be on it. They only had information on the committee's goal or task. Thus, the children were not able to segregate themselves by choosing a committee composed of others of the same sex and race.

A rapidly growing body of literature suggests that cooperative interdependence in attaining valued goals can lead to improved race relations. Perhaps one reason for this finding is that cooperative interdependence can lay the groundwork for a strong sense of group identity which cuts across racial lines. Such an identity is fostered by both the sharing of experience and mutual pride in the group's accomplishment.

The dues chart committees illustrate well the way in which the committee structure led to cooperative interdependence between black and white children. In their early meetings, the students voted to charge dues of 25 cents a month to all 150 students and 5 teachers on Team Z. Record-keeping was done by the several dues chart committees. A chart was constructed for each of the five homerooms on the team. While the basic format of the chart was the same for each class, each group was free to add designs (flowers, scrolls, etc.) and to select their own colors. Since making each chart involved design decisions as well as much printing and art work, students on the various dues chart committees were strongly impelled by the nature of their task to work together to achieve an end result they valued.

Jim, who is black, and Alex, who is white, sit down at a table with construction paper and pencils. Quickly, they realize that they'll need a ruler to pencil straight lines. Jim leaves and returns with a yardstick. They are soon joined by a black female, Debbie. She watches them drawing for a few moments and then suggests they write the names in pencil first, and then color over with crayon. They think this is a good idea. Jim tells Mark that he should write the names in pencil. Then Jim will color over them. Debbie offers additional suggestions about how to mix the colors of the letters, so that each first and last name is in a different color. The boys smile at her with approval while they look at the example she drew. She then rises from her chair and says that their sign "looks very nice." The boys are clearly pleased.....

Perhaps the most clear cut indication of the development of a sense of group identity which transcended racial lines was the change that occurred in the seating patterns in the student council. Field notes taken during each meeting described these patterns. Initially, the girls generally sat together, grouping themselves by race. Boys also tended to sit near other boys. Their seating pattern was not so obviously segregated by race but they still did cluster by race quite frequently. By the end of January,

> The kids are sitting in a kind of random pattern today... Girls and boys are mixed together and blacks and whites are sitting together too. There is no congregation of females in any particular corner as there often used to be.

This pattern continued for the remaining months, especially during the early part of each meeting in which the agenda items were discussed.

Although the very marked shift in seating patterns was obvious to the eye, there were other more subtle indications of the development of a strong positive group identity which transcended racial and sexual identities. A sense of group pride was evident in the kind of praise and approval students gave to each other -- applause and cheers -- when council officers reported on the status of different projects.

Involvement with and enthusiasm for the group was typified in the students' reactions to the idea of a student council organized talent show. The idea for this project came from council's suggestion box, which had been made by a committee and designed in the school colors. The show was written, directed, and organized by the council, but any student on Team Z who wanted to present an act was included. One of the first items for decision concerned organizing a committee to produce the show. Ms. Baker asked who would like to be in the show, and every single student raised his or her hand. To this, Ms. Baker responded,

"...All right. We need... an announcement to sign up people. I think the first question that we should ask is whether the talent show should be for all of the seventh grade or only Team Z?"...A chorus of students in unison responded: "Only Team Z..."

This project was a major undertaking, involving much administration and coordination. Students had to find a room that would accomodate about 150 people which would also have a dressing room. The various acts had to be timed and shortened if they were too long. A mistress or master of ceremonies had to be selected as did the judges, a production director, and a stage manager. The students had to decide on prizes and on whether or not to video tape the show, etc. Each of the thirty-three members of the Student Council directly participated in some aspect of the very successful production.

The effect of the student council on Team Z did not go unnoticed by others. During an interview, a seventh grade teacher on a team which did not have a student council was asked about the kinds of relations that had developed among black and white students attending Wexler. The first topic the teacher chose to discuss was the development of a feeling of belonging among the students.

> One of the things I'm concentrating on personally is building up this feeling of belonging. That probably could be a very important deed... Ms Baker and others (on Team Z) set up this program. They were sending cards to everybody on the team...who missed more than five days, or whom they knew was hurt or in the hospital or whatever. They planned talent shows and this kind of thing. It's the kind of thing that through loyalty to a group like a team, almost like a group of athletes... The blacks and whites, simply because they belonged to the same group, the same team, break down some of the resistance...

In conclusion, our analysis suggests that the student council promoted a strong sense of group identity and loyalty shared by black and white students alike. Contributing importantly to the development of this feeling were numerous factors including the rather special group roles and norms which fostered the cooperative interdependence students experienced in their committee work and the teacher's emphasis on unity and sensitivity to each other's feelings. The students worked together in the pursuit of common goals, and they had fun doing it. They had moments when committee work was finished in which they could read books together, or sit and talk, or even tease one another, arm wrestle or throw the occasional wad of paper in the direction of an unsuspecting friend or foe. They did all of these things. What they did not do was to ignore each other. Society, neighborhood, school and home all contribute in their own way to telling Wexler's students who they are and under what conditions they will live. These students are very conscious of themselves as interrelated social beings who live in a world that appears to them to be constructed and defined by the rules of the adult world. But for a time, they tended to act together on the basis of their commonality in being student council members, part of a team in the real sense of the word.

*The research on which this paper is based was funded by the first author's contract with the National Institute of Education.

All opinions expressed herein are solely those of the authors, and no endorsement of the ideas by BIE is implied or intended. The authors wish to express their deep appreciation to the students and staff of Wexler School for making this research possible.

SOURCES

Aronson, Eliot, Bridgeman, Diane, & Geffner, Robert, "The effects of a cooperative classroom structure on student behavior and attitudes." In D. Bar-Tal & L. Saxe, *Social Psychology of Education*. Washington, D.C.: Halsted Press, 1978.

Ashmore, Richard, "The problem of intergroup predudice." In B. Collins, *Social Psychology*. Menlo Park, California: Addison-Wesley, 1970.

Billig, Michael, *Social Psychology and Intergroup Relations*. New York: Academic Press, 1976.

Brigham, John, "Views of black and white children concerning the distribution of personality characteristics." *Journal of Personality*, 1974, 42, 145-168.

Doise, Willem, & Sinclair, Anne "The categorization process in intergroup relations." *European Journal of Social Psychology*, 1973, 3, 145-157.

Johnson, David, & Johnson, Roger, *"Instructional goal structure: Cooperative, competitive or individualistic."* Review of *Eucational Research*, 1974, 44, 213-240.

Katz, Phyllis, "The acquisition of racial attitudes in children." In Phyllis Katz (Ed.), *Toward the elimination of racism*. New York: Pergamon Press, 1976.

Noblit, George, & Collins, Thomas, *Desegregated education in Cross-Over High School*. Unpublished manuscript, Sociology Department, Memphis State University, 1977.

Patchen, Martin, Hofmann, Gerhard, & Davidson, James, "Interracial perceptions among high school students." *Sociometry*, 1976, 39(4), 334-354.

Pettigrew, Thomas, "Racially separate or together?" *Journal of Social Issues*, 1969, 25(1), 43-68.

Rist, Ray, "Race, policy and schooling." *Society*, 1974,

12 (1), 59-63.

Schofield, Janet, *"Competitive and complementary identities: Racial and gender identity in pre-adolescents.* In S. Asher and J. Gottman (Eds.), book in preparation, 1979.

Schofield, Janet, & Sagar, H. Andrew, *"Peer interaction patterns in an integrated middle school,"* Sociometry, 1977, 40, 130-138.

Schofield, Janet, & Sagar, H. Andrew, *"Unplanned social learning in an interracial school."* In Ray Rist (Ed.), *Desegregated schools: Appraisals of an American experiment.* New York: Academic Press, forthcoming.

Tajfel, Henri, *"Experiments in intergroup discrimination."* Scientific American, November, 1970, 223 (5), pp. 96-102.

9

OREO - MARGINAL MAN AND WOMAN

By

Charles Vert Willie

From *Oreo--On Race and Marginal Men and Women* by Charles V. Willie (Wakefield, MA. 01880: Parameter Press). © Charles V. Willie 1975. All rights reserved. Used by permission of and special arrangement with the publisher, Parameter Press, Inc.

The Oreo cookie became for me a "piece of finite reality," in the words of Paul Tillich. It was a bearer of something beyond itself; it was the medium for a holy encounter, "a medium of revelation." The Oreo cookie is a thick, double chocolate wafer with white cream filling in the middle. The coloring is brown and white and brown again.

LIKE IT IS IN THE WASHINGTON PROVINCE

In mid-June of 1969 at Hood College in Frederick, Maryland, the Washington Province of the Episcopal Church convened its annual conference. The Washington Province includes all or parts of the states of Pennsylvania, West Virginia, Delaware, Maryland, Virginia, and the District of Columbia. The theme for the conference was, "Like It Is and Like It Will Be." I was engaged as the morning lecturer to tell it like it is. The Rev. Herbert J. Ryan, S.J., had the responsibility of forecasting how it will be.

It was not my morning lectures, however, that were the turning point for the conference. Rather, the Oreo cookie emerged as a symbol both of racial separation and of racial integration at the Hood Conference. What happened demonstrated that actions speak louder than words. It is for this reason that I have urged many who call themselves religious, compassionate, humane, or civilized to focus as much upon actions as upon attitudes.

Let us get on with the story and the unfolding events. I was invited to be the morning lecturer for the conference. My wife, Mary Sue, and I arrived on the tree-lined campus of Hood College on a hot and humid Sunday afternoon in time for dinner and the Sunday evening Eucharist.

In terms of our conventional way of classifying people, I am black and my wife is white. In the Washington Province of the Episcopal Church, especially at a conference in Frederick, Maryland, race is always a significant variable, particularly when it involves male and female. I tell you these facts because they are related to the symbol of the Oreo cookie and the racial encounter which it mediated.

Early Monday morning at 8:30 a.m. I began my lecture by outlining a series of five topics related to the conference theme. The proposed series included (1) The Twofold Mission of the Church in the World, (2) Impediments to Effective Church Action, (3) The Interdependent Community, (4) The Anti-community Force: Separatism, and (5) The Black Manifesto: A Strange Cry for Redemption, an Urgent Call for Repentance. The actual topics and sequence of lectures were changed following the episode of the Oreo cookie midway through the conference.

In addition to the 45-minute lecture each morning, the conference was organized into several institutes that met daily and dealt with special subjects like church music, politics, revolution in the church, black and white relations, and Christian education. Each institute had a regular leader and visiting lecturers. The institute on black and white relations generated a great deal of anxiety. On the one hand, there was the coming together of black and white people to discuss America's most obvious failure, our own inability to get along with persons of different races; and, on the other hand, there was the coming together of younger and older people, trying to do business with each other in spite of the generation gap. This institute bore the burden of the racial and age separations and their characteristic estrangements.

I might add that the entire conference confessed its fault on the matter of age segregation and did something about it. Younger people -- high school youth and young adults -- were not separated from the main conference as in the past. They were part of the mainstream and participated in all the sessions.

For more than twenty years, The Hood Conference has been racially integrated. In fact, the conference was moved from

Virginia to Maryland a few decades ago so that black and white people could attend. The conference included men and women, although men were a minority of all participants.

The conference opened with the components of an explosive America interacting as if they were defused. In time, sweet harmony evaporated and exposed the divisions that persisted.

By Wednesday morning, I had worked my way through the topics about church mission and the impediments to church action. A warm appreciative applause followed each lecture. The meaning of such action is never clear. Is one being thanked for entertaining the audience, for confirming individuals' existing ideas, for not upsetting the people, or for telling it like it is? The Wednesday morning reaction was very much like that of the days before. But the substance of my lecture was a bit different. In addition to the analysis of the current social situation, I expressed a series of judgments:

1. that the most important capacity to cultivate in the professional leadership of the church is the capacity to develop maintain, and enhance community;

2. that a worshiping congregation that is a worshiping community must deliberately draw all sorts and conditions of people into the fellowship of the faithful; and

3. that the continued existence of all-white and all-black congregations is a blasphemous tragedy of contemporary civilization.

All this was said Wednesday morning in a lecture on the Interdependent Community.

By Wednesday noon, the divisions had emerged and were rotating on a black-white axis that intersected in the dining hall after lunch. An announcement over the public address system was made by a black priest. He said in jest that a revolution was about to start and that a black caucus was to be held in the end of the dining hall immediately after lunch. Of course, the purpose for the black caucus was not stated publicly. Later, someone said that it was called to recommend black candidates for the Board of Directors of the Hood Conference. However, the caucus never got down to business. Shortly after the caucus met, it was dismissed by the clergyman who had announced the assembly.

THE BLACK CAUCUS

The first person to crash the black caucus was a white woman whose husband is a priest who was scheduled to serve a predominantly black congregation. I suppose this is why she went to the caucus. Earlier, after the morning lecture, I had talked with this white conference member about her personal concerns and worries surrounding the new venture that she and her husband were about to undertake. I talked with her about the impossibility of avoiding mistakes; about the capacity which people who have to forgive, especially the capacity of people who have been oppressed. I said that, once she had been forgiven for a mistake, the basis for a real relationship would be laid. I then wished her well in her new involvement with a different kind of parish life in a predominantly black community. I suppose this white conference member felt she belonged in the black caucus. A few black people did not see it that way; they did not know of her circumstances. It might not have mattered even if they had known who she was and what her husband was about to do. So they demanded that she leave. She insisted that she must stay. This was only the first argument. Others were to follow immediately.

When I had been at lunch, a white tablemate insisted that the calling of the black caucus was discrimination and wanted to know what to do about it. I said, in conversation at the table, that black people and any people have the right to pursue the withdrawn if their pursuit is based on love, is an expression of genuine need for others, is a desire to share their burdens, and is an attempt to fulfill their needs. I provided some information that I had recently learned about two black men at the conference -- a laymen and a clergyman from Pennsylvania.

They had attended nearly twenty of these conferences in the past. In fact, the summer conference of the Washington Province of the Episcopal Church had been moved to Hood College largely because of the hot pursuit of these two men and other black people who knew that they were interdependent with white people and needed the experience of a summer church conference. It was because they had persisted in applying for admission to the all-white summer conferences more than twenty years before that Hood Conference is now interracial.

Thus the separatist movement among whites within the church, I explained, had been broken up by blacks who knew that the world was interdependent and that they and the whites needed each other. I then suggested that the separatist movement among blacks would be needed only if whites could admit that they needed blacks and therefore would pursue them in a spirit of love and interdependence.

Such pursuits were risky, I cautioned my listeners. The result might be that whites would experience some of the same kinds of insults that blacks had experienced years ago as they pursued whites who had insisted on maintaining racially segregated organizations and who openly stated that blacks were unwanted. Now blacks are saying similar things. Now whites must make a similar move for interdependence, a move that is based on love but that involves a risk to personal comfort.

Lunch was finished and the conversation ended. My wife and I arose to go to the black caucus, not knowing that another white person was already there. We did not issue the invitation, but two other white women from our luncheon table decided to go to the caucus with us. I don't know if they were with fear; but one woman was literally trembling.

The call for a caucus along racial-lines was a call that created a problem. But whose problem was it -- the problem of a black and white couple or the problem of a black or white caucus? In the Scriptures it is written, "...a man shall leave his father and mother and be joined to his wife, and the two shall become one" [Ephesians 5:31]. "What therefore God hath joined together, let no man put asunder"[Matthew 19:6], not even a black or white caucus. Where I go, there also may go my wife as we cleave to each other as one flesh.

But some members of the caucus didn't see it that way. The question is: Does family unity take precedence over racial unity? My wife and I affirm that it does.

So we approached the black caucus hand in hand. Attention focused on us as we approached the caucus, whose members were standing at one end of the dining hall.

"What are you doing here!" someone shouted at my wife.

"She is my wife!" I responded.

Then attention was turned to the two white women who came with us.

"Why are they here!" said the crowd.
"They are my friends!" I retorted.
"They have no right to be here!" was the angry reply.
"They are human beings," I said. "This is a caucus of human beings; let's get on with the meeting!"

One black man yelled that the humanity of whites was a debatable point. I told him that such a conception of race and humanity was his problem, not ours. Later I learned that the man who questioned the humanity of whites in the heat of argument is a clergyman. As the exchange became more intense, the other clergyman, who had convened the caucus sensed a deteriorating situation.

"Caucus dismissed," he declared.

THE SIGN ON THE SHEET

By accident, chance, or intuition, I already had announced the topic for the next day -- a discussion of the Black Manifesto. The topic had been shifted from Friday to Thursday. Moreover, I had requested that the Manifesto and the Response of the Executive Council of the Episcopal Church to the Manifesto be duplicated so that all might read them overnight. My plan was to distribute these documents after dinner.

Mine was not the only after-dinner plan. Someone decided to retaliate for the noontime confrontation. A sign on the sheet had been painted, a sign about the conference morning speaker. It read,

Dr. Willie is an Oreo Cookie

Beside these words was the likeness of that cookie -- dark brown (or black) on the outsides and white on the inside. The sign then suggested a course of action; it called for a boycott of the Thursday morning lecture. The sign was positioned above the door to the hall in which the evening lecture was to be presented. The sheet sheltered the doorway like a curtain so that all had to pull it aside to go through, so that all would be encouraged to read it.

The idea for a sign came from a young black woman who lived in the District of Columbia. At the time, I did not know her. First I read the sign. Then I inquired about who the author was. I wanted to know why that person was displeased. Also I wanted to defend my actions and explain the feelings that I had. But the author of the sign did not come forward until an annoyed conference member ripped it down.

Meanwhile, as the sign danced in the breeze, my wife and I retaliated. We stood behind the sign by the doorway and handed out documents for the next day's session, copies of the Black Manifesto and of the Response by the Executive Council of the Episcopal Church. We could have distributed these documents elsewhere in the building. But we decided to confront the sign if not its author and to overcome what was supposed to be an insult. Our presence and the sign were excitement. It was clear that the noontime drama had not ended. Indeed, the tension was escalating, and the outcome was in doubt.

My wife drew courage and strength from the adverse situation and determined that events should run their full course. Thus she held high the sign of the Oreo cookie for late arrivals to see, since it had been pulled down earlier by a conference participant. I continued to hand out the documents. The intended insult was becoming a farce. This was too much for the author to tolerate. She came forth and snatched the banner from the hands of my wife, insisting that it was her property. My wife was hurt by this act of hostility and rejection and momentarily lost her composure. She was comforted by other conference members and made a rapid recovery.

THE DESIRE FOR SEPARATISM

The designer of the sign, having revealed herself, was pursued by me for questioning. She was an attractive black teenager from Washington. I wanted to find out her reasons for insisting on racial separation. I tried to set forth some points in favor of integration. I became adamant in discussing the right of my wife to be with me no matter what coloring any caucus might be. The young woman spoke of the need for black people to be alone so that they could find their own identity. I informed the sign maker that her separatist ideology could lead to a bloody end that she might not be prepared to experience, for only by violence would my wife and I be separated. Those who insist on calling racial caucuses must be prepared to accept the inseparable couples whose members might be of different races. I wanted to impress upon this young person that the call for segregation was not a game. An adult black woman stood with the youthful conference member as we talked. She allowed that a white wife of a black husband should be accepted, but she insisted that other whites should have left the black caucus when they were ordered to do so. She termed "arrogant" their arguments against leaving.

To provide historical perspective, I pointed out that the Washington Province Conference probably was very uncomfortable when blacks insisted on attending years ago. I explained that, because blacks had insisted on disturbing whites out of their comfortable segregation in the past, the possibility for an interracial confrontation was present today. I concluded that blacks who insisted on maintaining segregation must now expect to be made similarly uncomfortable, for the world and its people are interdependent. None can make it on his or her own. Shortly thereafter, the evening session began with Father Ryan leading the discussion. We had to break off our conversation unfinished.

THE NEED FOR PERSPECTIVE

I worked hard that night on the next morning's lecture. It would be difficult to heal the broken hearts, especially since my behavior was a factor in the estrangement. Someone was needed to provide a perspective. I considered this to be my major task. Some black youths were bitter about the black caucus that had been crashed by whites. Some white adults were angered and insulted by the language used by blacks in the Manifesto. My responsibility was to deal with both issues in a way that would be helpful to all. My mission was nearly impossible. Yet I thought I should give it a try.

I read, I thought, and I wrote. I wished desperately for solitude and serenity to help the process of meditation and the sorting out of feeling from fact.

Suddenly there was a knock at my door. I answered. There stood a white youth, seeking me out in behalf of his friends. My thought and preparation were interrupted as I accepted his summons to come to the basement below to meet with a group of white teenagers.

They wanted to talk about the events of the day. There was nothing in particular they wanted to say except that they thought I had been treated unfairly. While sympathy seemed to be in short supply and I was delighted to receive even a little, I knew that more was at stake than merely my bruised feelings.

This was not a time to be sentimental. So I drew out the young people to learn of their feelings about race relations and what they thought ought to be done. They admitted that prejudice was present in this land and blamed their parents, more or less. Then we talked about why the black youth in the conference felt a need to emphasize their racial difference rather than their common humanity. The issue was translated into boy-girl terms so that the conclusion would have a major impact. I asked the young people if they had known some girls who were so insecure about their humanity that they felt the need always to relate to others in terms of their femininity. Most students admitted that they had known such persons. The principle was extended to the black youth. Maybe they felt a need to emphasize their race because they did not feel accepted as human beings, I suggested.

Then we talked about the responsibility of accepting. A few young people said they believed in meeting the other person halfway. Special circumstances of a relationship in love might require that one person go, not halfway, I reminded the young people, but all of the way to meet and reach another. Moreover, a special obligation was on the majority or the dominant people of power to over-extend themselves to the minority or the people with less power. I restated a principle that I had mentioned earlier in the conference that, from those unto whom much is given, more is required. Also, I talked about the need for whites to pursue blacks in a spirit of love and interdependence because, alone, whites stand incomplete. Such pursuit was a risky venture, however, and might result in some minor or major discomforts; but in the end it would be worth the effort.

Finally, I brought out that race and clan were of limited relevance in classifying individuals, that their humanity is what really matters. The outstanding task, as I saw it, was for the white youth to approach and accept the black youth as human beings so that the blacks could experience the irrelevance of race and not have to relate to others with race uppermost in their minds.

THE SIGN ON THE PIPE

Meanwhile, some of the white youths were preparing another sign as our discussion about race continued. Around a pipe that extended through the basement and hung near the ceiling, they had wrapped several squares of paper and were printing a large letter on each square. I could see that it said something about a cookie. When finished, the simple message read

BROTHERHOOD IS AN OREO COOKIE

That message remained up throughout the night and until the end of the conference. It was an important idea to remember. These youths had turned a symbol of insult and alienation into one of support and reconciliation. Indeed the healing process began that night among the young as well as the old.

The last hour of the day was rapidly approaching. I still had work to do. Black youths were slowly wandering into the hall for the late-night snack of chili. The white youths were already there. I sensed that something dramatic might happen that night. I thought it best to be on my way. So I excused myself from the seminar session and went to my room to write.

Then a real confrontation took place. Screaming and crying, the black girl who had designed the original Oreo cookie banner shouted out.

"Why should I ever trust white people? They always hurt me, and you will too! That's why we don't have anything to do with you!"

"But I'm not just 'white people,' I'm me! I'm a person, and I don't want to hurt you!" one of the white boys answered her in a loud voice.

The confrontation was intense and went on as a shouting match for nearly half an hour. It was the last confrontation that the young people experienced. After that, they began to draw together to plan a service of Holy Communion for the entire conference for Thursday night. They were beginning to turn toward each other.

While the confrontation was taking place between black and white youths, adults were meeting in small interracial groups in dormitory rooms all over the campus, talking into the wee hours of the morning, trying to deal with the hostilities of that day and their anger that had been generated by the Manifesto, trying to explain their feelings of oppression, trying to find a plausible explanation, trying to capture a bit of understanding. Yes, the reconciling process had begun.

Thursday morning, the lecture was almost anticlimatic. Participants had found many of the answers themselves. My major function was to talk about the Manifesto and also to put the episode of the Oreo cookie in proper perspective. I mentioned how, in fewer than six hours, a symbol of separation and division had evolved into a symbol of integration and unity. I suggested that Hood Conference '69 might be remembered as the Conference of the Oreo Cookie. The cookie was symbolic of so much. It pointed toward the brokenness and estrangement in human society and the eternal possibility of reuniting.

RECONCILIATION

The remainder of the day was uneventful. An attitude of anticipation prevailed, though, for all that was to come, for the known and unknown that had become a part of this conference.

After dinner and the evening lecture, the young people did their thing. The liturgy was new and different. There were strumming guitars and strange-sounding records. But most of all there was a warm embrace for all.

After Holy Communion, the youngsters flipped back to a fine Jewish expression -- *Shalom*. For nearly thirty minutes, conference members wandered around the room kissing and embracing each other and shouting, *"Shalom!"* It was a happy, joyful occasion and a wonderful lift from a period of strife.

There were black and white people, men and women, northerners and southerners, the young and the old, hugging and kissing each other. Some may have thought it silly. But most people acted as if it were sacred to let loose and express their love for one another. Toward the end of the period of celebration, I sought out the designer of the first sign and placed a kiss upon her cheek. The original sign had disappeared. Only the brotherhood sign remained as the conference continued to unite.

A new topic was needed for the Friday morning lecture, not the one I had planned to present. I talked about repentance, redemption, and reconciliation. Also, I dealt with the function of conflict.

"Members of most communities," I said, "yearn for a sweet and harmonious situation of peaceful cooperation. But often we cannot reach the stage of peaceful cooperation without first going through the turbulence of conflict or confrontation. It is well that we learn to endure it in love. This is the lesson that this conference has taught us."

A preacher from Pennsylvania summed up the conference this way: "By Friday at the closing Liturgy, the whole drama had been acted out, and the degree of reconciliation was beautiful. The black youth and the white youth were holding each other and laughing; they were together." He said that the message of hope and reconciliation had been acted out in a way that couldn't be put into words. The adult woman who had supported the angry black teenager embraced Mary Sue and me at the closing worship service, which was held out of doors on the campus. I was deeply moved by her expression of affection.

Oreo cookies were distributed. A man from Pennsylvania wanted to break bread together. He offered a piece of his Oreo cookie. I took it and ate it in grace.

"It was so beautiful," the preacher said. "It was so beautiful." I am persuaded to believe that it was.

SOURCES

Tillich, Paul, *Biblical Religion and the Search for Ultimate Reality*, Chicago: University of Chicago Press, 1955.

INTRODUCTION TO PART FOUR

PERSONAL BONDS

Personal bonds serve the needs of individuals rather than being a means toward some other end. The rules and restrictions of societies are never strong enough to prevent personal bonds from developing between individuals who find themselves emotionally attached to "strangers." Yet, closeness between people, always difficult to achieve, becomes doubly problematic when it lacks a nurturing atmosphere.

The three essays in our final section deal with three types of interracial personal bonds--man-woman, parent-child, and woman-woman.

June True theorizes about a black man-white woman love and sexual attraction from the viewpoint of a sociologist who is a white woman, dealing critically with the theories of social scientists and the stereotypes of the public.

Adoptive parents face many questions, but very important is the issue of truthfulness about the situation of adoption. Those who adopt transracially have other serious problems, but not this one. Joyce Ladner, another sociologist, raises the question of whether, in a society which emphasizes color, white parents can recognize and meet the challenge of helping to create a positive racial identity for their transracially adopted children. She presents the arguments of those who oppose and those who favor such adoptions.

Finally, we end the book on a positive note--presenting the personal narratives of Gloria Orenstein and Adah Askew about their friendship and how it grew. Both were drawn to an interracial cooperative in New York as the setting in which they wanted to raise their children. As each asserted her quest for intellectual excitement and for a role in the world outside the home, she found a steady source of support in the other. Similar interests and problems overshadowed vastly different origins and brought them increasingly closer. Unashamedly and yes, somewhat sentimentally, they celebrate their bonds of friendship.

10

MISS ANNE AND THE BLACK BROTHER

By

June A. True

This paper is about the most explosive issue in the long confrontation between blacks and whites, the most mentioned and least understood of all black-white relations. This paper is about sex, love, and marriage between black brothers and the white man's caucasian sisters.

The importance of this topic lies in the emphasis given it by exaggerating racists and minimizing liberals. Both respond hysterically to the idea of interracial love and sex, promoting irrational attitudes and behavior, the first through fear of unlikely events, and the second through denial of real ones.

Although members of both sexes in both races have crossed the color line, this discussion will concentrate on the pairing of black men and white women for two reasons, the disproportionate attention paid to it being one of them. The other is less obvious.

Much has been written about the attitudes of white men toward interracial sex between "their" women and black men. Quite a few publications discuss black men and women's attitudes also. Writers from all three categories have published their views. Practically nothing has been heard from white women, except for a few journalistic observations on miscegenation. Since the present writer is a white woman, this paper is a contribution toward filling that gap.

INTERRACIAL SEX AS A FOCUS FOR RACIST ANGER

In 1963, Brink and Harris conducted a survey on white attitudes towards blacks. They were struck by the "violent emotionalism" and the "element of fear" contained in the white responses. They commented that, "this wall of white emotion is the real enemy of the Negro revolution." Negative remarks by whites specifically mentioned sex, in or out of marriage.

The idea that integration equals interracial sex has been prominent in the rhetoric of the segregationists from the beginning. Even so, very few are as blatant as the National States' Rights Party press, which warns with screaming capital letters that integrated schools will lead immediately to the MONGRELIZATION OF THE RACE. Prevalent among the polished are the "reasoned" discussions of practical reasons any sensible black person would have for wanting to marry us. These range from improving the chances of one's offspring to raising one's own rank. Less-polished types speak of criminal or animal drives, or revenge. John Dollard, in *Caste and Class in a Southern Town* says that fear of revenge causes white men to project their own lust for women of another race onto the black men.

Claims that blacks are sexually interested in whites contain two consistent assumptions. The first is that the desire is exclusively male, and the second is that no sane white will return it. Whites who have crossed the line are classified as feeble-minded, degenerate, or delinquent. Black women do not stand accused of wanting white men, even though there is evidence that some do. The black male alone is pictured as a dangerous sexual aggressor, moving against a demurring, defenseless, white woman.

BLACK OPINION

Black spokesmen used to deny that blacks wanted intermarriage. Dr. W.E.B. DuBois stressed that anti-intermarriage laws were unacceptable only because they left black women helpless "before the lust of white men," and because they implied black inferiority. Many writers declared that the intermarriage issue was raised only to justify exploitation. More recently militant writers have openly discussed black male interest in white women. Some refer to it as an aberration of the past, some as a social or economic expedient, some as a manifestation of psychiatric problems. It wasn't until 1972 that Beth Day, writing in *Sexual Life Between Black and Whites* could refer to half a dozen cautiously favorable statements by black leaders and writers on the subject of love and marriage between the races.

All of those statements were by black men. Recent writings by black women is full of admonitions and warnings to the black man, exhorting him to give up white women. Only Toni Cade sees a transitional function in a black male-white female union. She believes that a man will become more militant if he has a white woman because his blackness will be constantly emphasized, until he leaves her and returns to the women he "should" pursue.

Maybe white men can't imagine a white woman welcoming a black man, but blacks have often commented that the white man must be afraid she might, or he wouldn't be so nervous about it. They correctly point out that the anti-miscegenation laws are aimed at enduring, voluntary relationships. Many times white women were punished for cohabiting with black men or for having their children. According to Lerone Bennett, in *Before the Mayflower*, there were always numerous candidates for this punishment. According to actress Abby Lincoln, there still are. While Bennett refrains from making a moral judgment, Lincoln accuses us of every unacceptable motivation from nymphomania to bigotry. She pinpoints the sexual superiority myth as the reason for our interest in black men.

This belief, that the black male is more adept sexually than the white male, permeates the writings of both races. Even psychiatrists William H. Grier and Price M. Cobbs, in *Black Rage*, claim that there is no other lover who can give us so much pleasure as the black man can--due to a combination of oedipal fantasies, repressed desire, and curiosity. Although these are not physiological reasons, and the good doctors are careful to explain that such liaisons must end in disaster, they do leave the impression that we couldn't do better sexually than to choose a black man.

THE MYSTERY WOMEN

With all this controversy raging over our heads, most of us have remained silent so far. Our recorded comments are confined

to descriptions of southern miscegenation past and present
(involving *other* white women), occasional complaints by the
women whose husbands have an eye for black women, and a few
defensive statements made by white women caught in the act with
a black man or dead-to-rights with a black baby. Dollard recognizes that we have not been heard from, but presents some skimpy
evidence that he could garner. He notes that we sometimes accept
black men, that some of us titter about black sexuality. Dr. Helena
Deutsch recorded the occurrence of sexual fantasies about black
men on the part of some of us.

After noting Dr. Deutsch's impression that white men were
reacting to the *psychic* reality of these fantasies as if to *physical*
reality, Dollard comments, "if this theory could be accepted"
it would throw much light on the reactions of white men to the
race issue. Doubtless it would. Doubtless it would also go far to
explain the surprising gaps in the literature on interracial sex.
Most of the work on black-white mating is purely speculative.
Some writers include fragmentary or impressionistic data. There
has been no systematic attempt to determine the attitudes or
opinions of white women on an issue in which we are the central
figures. When I searched the literature in preparation for my
1970 survey on white attitudes towards blacks, I could find no
study which bothered to separate the responses of whites by sex.
Recently there has been some interest in determining the opinions
of white women, but the scientific study of interracial sex and
marriage in general, has barely begun. The subject of *love*
between the races has been addressed only by novelists and
playwrights.

THE CASE OF THE LOP-SIDED MARRIAGE PATTERN

The only hard data we have on interracial pairings is marriage
data. There are scattered records from the seventeenth century
on, in this country. All but one, that I have been able to discover,
show a preponderance of marriages between black men and white
women. That one was Constantine Panunzio's Los Angeles study
and it mainly concerned black women and Asian men in an area
in which intermarriage was forbidden. Another dissenting voice
is that of the Census Bureau. Their figures show roughly equal

proportions of marriages between white men and black women and marriages between black men and white women, at least for recent decades.

There are a number of possible explanations for the impression that black male-white female pairings are the predominant phenomena. It's possible that this combination is selectively perceived; that white male-black female couples live in sin, (reporting themselves as married to the census-taker); that one type is available to researchers and the other not. Regardless of the explanation, it is of slight interest to the issue of black-white sex relations. Sex between people is the focus of concern, especially sex between black men and white women, and whether or not it is legalized is of no moment for present purposes. We must attend to both marriage and extra-marital affairs. Furthermore, it is not significant if white women and black men want each other more than black women and white men. The only thing that signifies is whether or not white women want black men at all, since this possibility is evidently what triggers racist outpourings.

THEORIZING MOTIVATION AND MOTIVATING THEORY

Focusing on *marriage* results in eliminating consideration of *private* motivations for interracial sex in favor of *public* motivations, since marriage is usually a public declaration of choice. This is especially likely because we tend to fall into the error of thinking that a single motivation explains our behavior. If someone's action can be explained by an obvious benefit, that is THE reason for it. Psychologists often go one better and bypass the overt benefit, seizing the covert benefit as THE reason. Let's see how one theorist, Robert K. Merton, analyzes interracial marriage, using a typically simplistic approach.

In his 1941 article, "Intermarriage and the Social Structure: Fact and Theory," Merton constructs a typology of all possible class-caste combinations, given two sexes, two (!) social classes, and two races. He discusses only the "deviant" cases, or racial intermarriages. There are eight possibilities:

1. Upper-class black woman + Upper-class white man
2. Upper-class white woman + Upper-class black man

3. Upper-class black woman + Lower-class white man
4. Upper-class white woman + Lower-class black man
5. Lower-class black woman + Upper-class white man
6. Lower-class white woman + Upper-class black man
7. Lower-class black woman + Lower-class white man
8. Lower-class white woman + Lower-class black man

Merton explains numbers 1 and 2 as instances of the rebellion and alienation of people who enjoy high status and are "emancipated" from our social norms. Numbers 7 and 8 are, in his view, people who can't make it socially anyway and have nothing to lose. After dismissing these four possible combinations, he concentrates on the four that cross socio-economic lines as well as racial ones.

Number 3, the marriage of an upper-class black woman to a lower-class white man, Merton feels is very unlikely, because the role of the male is that of economic provider. He expects that Number 5, involving lower-class black women and upper-class white men, will be frequent, and comments several times that it *has* been, but feels that legal marriage will be rare, most couples practicing concubinage instead. This he attributes to the poor bargaining power of the black woman.

The marriage of an upper-class black man to a lower-class white woman is the most likely interracial pairing, in Merton's eyes. He points out that the woman in this marriage is exchanging her superior social standing for her husband's superior economic standing. Number 4, the marriage of an upper-class white woman to a lower-class black man is extremely unlikely, Merton claims, because the woman's only possible motivation would be sex.

Note that Merton's analytic stance shifts constantly, and contains a number of unsubstantiated assumptions. (Remember also, that this "study" contains *no data* to back up the theory). Numbers 3 and 5 are regarded from the perspective of the *white* male and numbers 4 and 6 from the perspective of the *white* female. Assumptions are as follows:

1. White men never marry black women for money.
2. White men usually marry/fornicate with black women for sex.
3. Black people accept/pursue white people for social advancement, including money.
4. White women marry black men for money.

5. White women are less sexually interested in black men than white men are in black women.

Note that everyone is for sale except the white man and everyone is marrying for reasons other than companionship and love. He fails to mention sexual interest of black people in whites and implies that white women are sexually indifferent. Observe how comfortably this analysis fits into the racist and liberal patterns!

We have very little evidence as to why interracial couples got married, except for scattered testimony and the census data, from which we can infer, at least, socio-economic standing. Jessie Bernard, in *Marriage and Family Among Negroes,* 1966, cites a study from Indiana, showing that the occupational distribution for 95 interracial couples was the same as that for the state as a whole. I analyzed the 1960 Census Report on interracial marriages and found that most intermarriages are contracted between people with similar education. I also found that when black men marry white women they are just as likely to be less educated than their wives as they are to be more educated.

Approaching the study of interracial sex by analyzing known cases as deviants has another effect. It avoids the question of the general attitude of white women toward blacks, and especially black men. It's easy then to say that we are dealing with the violation of a taboo by social failures and crackpots. It's easy to sidestep the white women's sexuality and the possibility that we might be attracted by black men. One writer who bluntly says that we are so attracted is the *British* sexual anthropologist Eric Dingwall, in *The American Woman,* 1957.

> The attraction that Latin men indubitably exercise over white women, and especially white American women, leads directly to the question as to how far white American women are attracted by Negro men...The belief (that) Negro men (like) white women is accompanied by the belief that, were white women allowed to know Negro men better, they would find them attractive. I have no doubt whatever that this is true....

Dingwall's opinion is that we are sexually unsatisfied and jealous of black women because our men pay attention to them, and that white men are jealous of black men due to the "common delusion" that they are more virile. He may be able to spot the black virility legend as a "common delusion" when it refers to black males, but not when it refers to black females.

>...the Negro woman was not only complaisant; she was free from that ever-present sense of guilt and sin which still permeates all American society. Thus, she offered a contrast to the white woman of the South...

Gunnar Myrdal in *An American Dilemma* says the belief in the black woman's "freedom" and easy virtue eases the white man's conscience and amounts to wishful thinking. Perhaps so. He says, too, that belief in black men's large genitalia and sexual prowess is partly envy and partly a *social control device* to prevent white women's congress with black men. It seems that large genitalia are considered to be sexually advantageous but that they will scare off white women. Evidently, we white women do not like what is presumed to be sexually advantageous. In short, we do not like sex!

John Dollard in *Caste and Class in a Southern Town,* discusses the white man's fear of retaliation, which he attributes to their guilt. He says they deny the possibility of white women's interest in black men because they cannot bear to face it. Another author, Charles Stember, in *Sexual Racism,* theorizes that the white man's sexual jealousy has another dimension. He believes that a man's sexual pleasure is actually enhanced by the degree of conquest he experiences. Since the perceived social distance between black men and white women is great, the conquest is great, and the sexual pleasure is great. The white men cannot possibly achieve this much of a conquest, since they have no group of women as far above them. Therefore, the black man is in a position to achieve more pleasure than the white man can ever have, and the white man is insanely jealous. This theory reveals racial prejudice to be primarily a male phenomenon. An interesting implication of Stember's theory is that the white man should be most jealous and, therefore, hateful when the white woman involved is of high status and also inaccessible to himself. The women most likely to meet these two criteria are his daughters, since they are inaccessible and have youthful high sexual status. To Stember, the question "would you want your daughter..." is the appropriate one.

To the question, "would your daughter want...?" Stember

replies "Yes." He feels that women are trained to respond to admiration and desire because their self-image depends on men's definitions of them. If black men want us more than white men do, we will sense this extra desire and respond to it. White men will understand this potential and react. In addition, their jealousy will be observed by black men, who get an extra sexual thrill because of it.

This theory has the merit of introducing the idea that white women are motivated by something other than money or insanity, but what Stember gives with one hand he takes away with the other. We are reduced to mindless automatons, blindly responding to whichever men want us the most. One wonders why we don't flock to accept other socially handicapped men, the stupid, the poor, the aged. Surely their conquest of us would be as sexually exciting to them and their desire correspondingly great. In fact, human beings, including women, often respond to those of the opposite sex who are downright indifferent.

Most white theorists are reluctant to admit that black people are attractive to white people, although they take the reverse phenomenon for granted. I will not belabor the point. It seems enough to say that a great amount of miscegenation has taken place, that black entertainers and athletes are the focus of great admiration among us, and that reports in the literature, professional and popular alike, give a great deal of information about our insatiable interest in our dark brothers and sisters. Attraction to each other is not in question. The thing that needs explanation is the *defiance* of society's taboo. The greater the taboo, the higher the motivation must be. Since the greatest taboo concerns black men and white women, let's try to see if we can find an extra motivation for them, all the while bearing in mind that motivation is many-sided, and we must not lose sight of the *basic* admiration and love involved.

WHITE VS. BLACK

General theory about anti-black feeling implies no sex difference in level of hostility. Sometimes race prejudice is explained as a biologically natural phenomenon. Sometimes it is termed a social expression of group solidarity, or a consciousness of kind. The "Christian" position has always been that it is the result of the curse of God upon Ham, son of Noah, for disrespecting his father. None of these makes room for any difference in prejudice between the sexes.

Sociological theory focuses on the *functions* of prejudice. Whites enjoy money, status, power, and sexual access to black women because of the exploitation of the blacks. Whites are guilty because they have benefitted unfairly, fearful of retaliation, frustrated if they fall below blacks in socio-economic status, authoritarian if they have "social anxiety," and sexually repressed, displacing lust onto the blacks. There is a good summary of this perspective in Simpson and Yinger's *"Racial and Cultural Minorities,"* 1965. While it is true that the sexual gains are only for white males, there is a balancing gain for females in that discrimination and segregation reduce the possibility that their children will drop in social status via intermarriage. Some theorists claim that women are more concerned with social status and family opportunities. (I'll have another look at that claim later.)

Some writers say that the avoidance patterns of the whites are prompted by the desire to keep the children away from unacceptable marriage partners and that other races are always classified as unacceptable. As we live in a mixed society, residential segregation becomes important. Note that if this claim is true, the presence and age of children should have some effect on the level of racial hostility.

Stember's theory implies a big difference in level of racial prejudice between the sexes. White women should be much more favorable to blacks and, in particular, to sex between black men and white women. While this author does not expect white women to discard prejudice completely, he maintains that they will differ from white males. The latter should be far more hostile toward interracial sex when the black partner is male than when the black partner is female.

Another implication of the Stember theory is that a white woman with a starved ego would be more responsive to black men than a woman who has received a lot of admiration. Sound familiar? Of course. It is a new variety of the old theory that rejected white women seek or accept black men. Merton said the same thing, but concentrated on socio-economic, rather than sexual, status.

THE GOALS OF WOMEN

Social science theory presents women's interests to be primarily love, social life, our own physical appeal, and clothes. Theodor Reik, in *Love and Lust*, says we are less secure than men and that is why we are more in need of love. E. M. Bennett and L. R. Cohen, in the article "Men and Women: Personality Patterns and Contrasts," found that men expected rewards and punishments for their own adequacy or lack of it, while we expected rewards and punishments based on others' attitudes. Talcott Parsons says that the youth culture confirms these expectations.

What women find attractive in men is also culturally prescribed. The young man must be prosperous. Some writers feel that this amounts to prostitution. Simone de Beauvoir, in the *Second Sex*, calls it a bribe. She says that society bribes us to agree to our own inferiority, by presenting marriage as the most honorable career; by forcing the married man to support his wife; by making unmarried motherhood difficult; by discouraging our attempts at personal achievement.

Marriage is presented to men as an advantage in life, but not as an alternative life style, competing with a useful paid occupation. A man takes economic responsibility for a woman, who surrenders her autonomy in order to enhance his. This passive role demands that woman must be what her man wants her to be. She must try to be beautiful, charming, helpful, admiring, supportive, *appropriately* sexy (according to his subcultural standards). He wants her competent, but not competitive; strong, but not dominant; well-organized without leading. She must achieve, but not too much. Two things happen. It becomes second nature to us to defer to men and to their definitions, and we learn to live through others. We become "feminine."

Living through others means that a single woman must attract a man with good prospects, because she will be part of him. *He* is her career until she has children and then the children become an outlet for her achievement, too. This is why social theorists claim that women are more concerned about neighbors, family status, and child protection in the social sense, than men are. The social science picture of women is that we see the world through men's eyes, defer to their opinions, and live their lives rather than our own. Greatly concerned about our children's opportunities, we are seen as protective towards them.

A CLOSER LOOK AT WOMEN'S NEEDS AND MOTIVES

Hegel has well said that women's ethic is impure. We are trained from birth to maneuver and scheme, the object being to trap a likely prospect into marriage. One of our ingrained personality traits is renunciation of self, and society will punish us for trying to overcome it. So, most women do not try. But, as Ralph Turner has said, taking the role someone else wants you to take may or may not involve adopting the viewpoint as your own. You can play the role but not be wholehearted about it.

One of the things men want women to do is to value what in a man corresponds to *his* need. *His* desires must sweep her off her feet, *his* passion must dissolve her resistance, *he* must conquer. Above all, she must not value him as means to an end. Even prostitutes pretend otherwise.

Observe how Stember's romantic theory that women respond to *a man's* perceived desire harmonizes with the male definition of women's role. Alas, it collides with two large chunks of reality. First, women cannot afford to make impractical choices until their important life goals have been reached. We *do* value men as means to an end, often clothing our particular prospect in romantic illusion to hide the practical considerations involved in the choice. This has been the pattern for centuries. Countless admonitions exist in literature, song, and story, warning us against the temptation to break that pattern and choose the "wrong" man.

Second, we do not respond to the intensity of a male's desire even if we are choosing among a group of men equal in good prospects. If we did, we wouldn't tire of a man unless someone else wanted us more.

The goals of women are to achieve those statuses established for us by society, namely, marriage and motherhood, preferably the motherhood of sons. Sexual selection must operate with reference to those goals. Unless we have a wide choice of potential spouses, all equally desirable *as spouses*, it is idle to speak of *sexual* selection at all.

With respect to our prescribed goals, the black man is not much competition as yet for the white man because his prospects are not as good. Like the British Tommy vis-a-vis American soldiers in World War II, he can't compete with men who have more money. At first glance, this might look as if the white man is worrying for nothing. But let's take a second glance at those female goals.

One important feature about marriage and motherhood is that they both confer an irreversible status rise. Once married, one can never again be an old maid. Once having borne a child, one can never be barren, even if the child eventually dies. The wedding ring and the child have a liberating effect. A wife and mother can be critical, outspoken, and even nagging, in a way which would ruin the chances of a spinster.

Another important feature about those goals is that they promised more than they will deliver. We were to gain approval and status benefits via marriage and motherhood, and the ego gratification which Stember rightly thinks is important to us (and to everyone). Gradually, as this ego gratification fails to materialize, we become discontent and frustrated. This discontent and frustration proceed out of our own unmet needs, not out of our husbands' waning desire. If we are to believe the writers on the subject, most wives think their husbands want too much sex, even though one of their unmet needs is sex. How can this be?

Although writers from Mark Twain to Dr. David Reuben have commented on our superior sexual capacity, we have never been permitted the indulgence of our sexual drives to the same extent as males. Formerly, we were not aware of our own sexual potential. (Of course, awareness is not a prerequisite for frustration.) We modern women usually know that we have an *unrealized* sexual potential, even though current role requirements *demand* that we appear to enjoy sex so that our partners can be termed successful lovers. We simply add another act to our repertoire and take on another measure of resentment and frustration with it. Sex remains something we give to the male for his enjoyment. (Or something withheld, as revenge.) Just as our sexual "purity" enhances us in the male's eyes, it places sex, for us, in the category of forbidden fruit. Fifty years of bowdlerized

Freud have not been sufficient to change this.

Parsons, in *Social Structure and Personality,* calls attention to another problem: the need to form a stable attachment to a person of the opposite sex, treating the other as an equal, not being dependent nor parental in attitude. De Beauvoir puts this a little differently.

> And doubtless she will encounter among them some who will not discourage her esteem...but she will be lucky if they make no show of arrogance...When she contemplates an affair...her problem is to find a man whom she can regard as an equal without his considering himself superior.

White women are hungry for two things we do not have: sexual satisfaction and recognition as adults. What is not generally perceived is that recognition as an adult (if you *are* an adult) is essential to sexual satisfaction. I think it is also a prerequisite to love. The black man and the white woman are in a position to offer this recognition to each other and, thanks to the white man's frantic efforts to keep us apart, can also offer the excitement of mystery. He is the symbol of sex, she of purity. He is a male who will give her first-class status, she is a white who will give him first-class status. It is an exchange that Merton did not anticipate, and it amounts to mutual respect, the basis of love. None of the theorists have considered this possibility because the same blind prejudice that prevents them from seeing our practical traditional motives for choosing a man also prevents them from seeing that new motives are possible *under changed conditions.* They sing that "love is her whole happiness" while we are grimly searching for a "suitable" man, and ignore the role of love when we select an "unsuitable" one.

I would expect that white women would be more likely to form liaisons of any kind with black men if:
1. They are or have been married.
2. They are mothers.
3. They are self-supporting.
4. They have a strong self-image and are not willing to settle for second-class status.

The first three eliminate the need to fulfill the traditional specifications. The fourth is more probable if the first three have been realized, but with today's changing social scene many women are reaching 3 and 4 without having to consider 1 and 2. In sum, I am saying that I think women will select men for companionship and love *whenever they are free to do so* and that black men are in a unique position to offer these to white women. If I'm right, research should show that white women are more favorable to black people, especially men, than white men are. If my theory about goal attainment is correct, white women who have been married and are mothers should be more favorable toward black people than women who remain single; independent women and women with good self-images should be more favorable than dependent women and women with poor self-images.

My doctoral dissertation, *The Sexual Basis of White Resistance to Racial Integration* (1971), reported an investigation of three questions: whether or not sex is a differentiating factor in white resistance to integration, whether or not the focus of sexual fears is the white female, and what factors, if any, are associated with differential male and female attitudes. The data were gathered by means of a two-page structured questionnaire administered to evening school students. The study population consisted of 716 white adults, of whom 490 were men and 226 were women. They were attending classes which fell into a random sample at two centers of University College, the evening division of Rutgers University. A comparison of the parameters of the study group with the general student body at University College showed that my sample was typical. They were mainly in their twenties and thirties and came from the middle and working classes. Four-fifths of the men were or had been married, as were two-thirds of the women. Three-quarters of the ever-married people had children then living at home. They had all, of course, completed high school. Since the sample was *not* a random sample of the United States, the data presented below cannot be used to generalize to the entire population, and no such attempt will be made. It is offered here only as an indication of what we might find if a more comprehensive study could be made.

Respondents were asked four questions about hypothetically integrated situations: Blacks moving into their neighborhood in large numbers; sending their children to a good school more than 50% black; their teenage children dating blacks; and a relative or close friend wanting to marry a black. The split ballot technique was used. There were two versions of the questionnaire. The first asked about a teenaged son dating a black girl and a male relative or friend wanting to marry a black. The second asked the same questions but about a teenaged daughter and a female relative or friend. The questionnaires were distributed alternately, so that half of the sample received a "male" questionnaire and half a "female" one.

Seventy-one per cent of the sample answered favorably about the "good" school in which over half of the students were black; 52% answered favorably about the integrated neighborhood; 51% about the marriage of a relative or close friend; and 31% about teenage dating. Differences between parents and childless people were small, parents being *slightly* less accepting of integration than non-parents. When we compare the responses of men with those of women, a big difference emerges. White women are more accepting on every issue and this held true whether I controlled for age, class, parenthood, marital status, religion, gender of black partner in dating or marrying, or attitudes toward roles of women. Differences between white men and white women ranged from 7% to 22% when they were not subdivided by any other variable. The differences were greatest on the questions about integrated neighborhoods and the dating and marriage of black males and white females. Space does not permit a presentation of detailed findings, but here are some basic conclusions:

1. White women are more favorable to integrated situations than are white men.
2. Whites in general are less negative about teenage dating for white boys and black girls than they are about dating for black boys and white girls.
3. White women do not repeat the above pattern for adult marriage; but white men do.
4. Fathers are less accepting of integrated neighborhoods and schools than mothers are.
5. Working-class men are more prejudiced than middle-class men against white women marrying black men, *but* class made no difference on this question for women.
6. Aging, marriage, and parenthood of sons are associated with more prejudiced responses among white men.
7. Aging, marriage, and parenthood of sons are associated with less prejudiced responses among white women.
8. Women who disagree with the traditional decision-

making role of husbands are less prejudiced toward white women marrying black men than are other white women.

You can see that, if these findings were to be duplicated in a nationwide survey, a lot of theory about whites' attitudes would have to be revised and the influence of gender on those attitudes would have to be taken into account. For example, women do not seem to be more protective toward children than men (item 4), nor less accepting of black men than of black women (item 3), nor more accepting of black men if they themselves are poor (item 5). Items 7 and 8 harmonized with my expectations, and item 6 was a bonus I failed to anticipate, although it seems logical, once considered. If (sexual) status security makes women more likely to speak their minds, there is no reason why it shouldn't work the same for men, and so it seems to do. The difference in percentage of favorable responses to the idea of black men marrying white women between white mothers of sons and white fathers of sons is 45%! Specifically, white mothers of sons were 77% unopposed to such marriages and white fathers of sons were 32% unopposed to them.

The only other survey I know which sheds any light at all on the difference between the attitudes of white women and white men toward blacks is the one done by Rhoda Goldstein, Thomas Slaughter and myself on Black Studies programs at colleges and universities in 1972. We found that all-female schools were more likely to have Black Studies programs and had them earlier than co-ed schools, and that co-ed schools were more likely to have them and had them earlier than all-male schools. I commented at the time, that, *in my opinion*, the more spirited and resourceful black (woman) was obviously winning her way when confronted with the more passive and less prejudiced white (woman).

WHAT DOES IT ALL MEAN?

We seemed to have reached the conclusion that freedom to speak one's mind would result in a simple pattern of prejudice, with each sex disapproving of interracial sex as competition but not as opportunity. Regardless of the white man's endless fascination with the question "would you want your daughter...?" it does not seem to be the appropriate one. It would be more relevant to ask "does the mother of your sons want...?"

What does this mean for the future? What does it mean for the white man's fear--which we have to consider since its consequences are so troublesome? I may seem to have arrived at the conclusion that the discarding of the masculinity/femininity mystique and with it, second class citizenship for me and my sisters, would result in a simple pattern of prejudice, where each sex would disapprove of interracial liaisons for the opposite sex and intensify this disapproval with age. If sexual attitudes underly social policy, the latter would become more negative all the time.

But, I have theorized earlier that white women may be *especially* attracted (in addition to normal, everyday liking) to black men for two reasons: promise of sexual fulfillment and promise of equal treatment. With the disappearance of male chauvinism, both reasons would be removed and replaced by free choice of individuals for their own sake. As marriage and the family become proportionately less important to women, we are more likely to achieve social recognition and sexual satisfaction. However, should the male chauvinist-feminist challenge remain strong and the blacks continue to advance socio-economically, the black man is a strong contender for white women. But should the blacks advance and the male chauvinist mystique crumble, interracial sex would settle at a rate harmonious with other intergroup rates: for the forces that determine pairing would then be the same as they are for all other combinations--proximity, social status, and opportunity.

The male chauvinist mystique cannot crumble unless the terrible fear of not being able to prove one's masculinity by "scoring" crumbles, too. The element of conquest will have to disappear and, with it, the need to compete for a prize instead of enjoying a shared pleasure. Meanwhile, those who are imprisoned within the present system will continue to seek and find each other.

SOURCES

Albert, June (True), Rhoda L. Goldstein and Thomas F. Slaughter, Jr. "The Status of Black Studies Programs at

American Colleges and Universities," Ch. 8 in *The Black Studies Debate*, J. U. Gordon and J. M. Rosser (eds.), Lawrence: University of Kansas, 1974.
de Beauvoir, Simone, *The Second Sex*, Tr. H. M. Parshley, New York: Knopf, 1952.
Bennett, E. M., and L. R. Cohen, "Men and Women: Personality Patterns and Contrasts," *Genetic Psychology Monographs*, Vol. 59, 1959, pp. 105-109; 147-153.
Bernard, Jessie, *Marriage and Family Among Negroes*, Englewood Cliffs, N.J.: Prentice Hall, 1966. Spectrum edition.
Brink, William, and Louis Harris, *Black and White*, New York: Simon and Schuster, 1967.
_____*"The Negro Revolution in America,"* New York: Simon and Schuster, 1963.
Cade, Toni, "Thinking About the Play 'The Great White Hope'," in Toni Cade (ed.), *The Black Woman*, New York: New American Library, 1970, pp. 237-243.
Day, Beth, *Sexual Life Between Blacks and Whites*, New York: World Publishing Co., 1972.
Dingwall, Eric John, *The American Woman*, New York: Rinehart, 1957, (London: Duckworth, 1956.)
Dollard, John, *Caste and Class in a Southern Town*, New York: Harper, 1949.
DuBois, W.E.B., *An ABC of Color*, New York: International Publishers, 1969.
Grier, William H., and Price M. Cobbs, *Black Rage*, New York: Basic Books, 1968
Basic Books, 1968.
Lincoln, Abby, "Who Will Revere the Black Woman?" in Toni Cade (ed.), *The Black Woman*, New York: New American Library, 1970, pp. 80-84.
Merton, Robert, "Intermarriage and the Social Structure," in *Psychiatry*, IV (August, 1941), pp. 362-374.
Myrdal, Gunnar, *An American Dilemma*, New York: Mc-Graw-Hill, 1962.
Panunzio, Constantine M., "Intermarriage in Los Angeles 1924-1933," *American Journal of Sociology*, XLVII (March, 1942), pp. 690-701.
Parsons, Talcott, *Social Structure and Personality*, London: Macmillan, 1963; (New York: Free Press of Glencoe, 1964.)
_____*The Social System*, New York: Free

Press of Glencoe, 1951.

Reik, Theodor, *Of Love and Lust; On the Psychoanalysis of Romantic and Sexual Emotions,* New York: Farrar, Strauss and Cudahy, 1957.

Simpson, George Eaton, and J. Milton Yinger, *Racial and Cultural Minorities,* New York: Harper and Row, 1965 (3rd ed.)

Stember, Charles H., *Sexual Racism,* New York: Elsevier, 1976.

Thunderbolt, The, Special Election Supplement, May, 1968.

Turner, Ralph H., "Role-taking, Role-standpoint, and Reference-group Behavior," in Bruce J. Biddle and Edwin J. Thomas, *Role Theory: Concepts and Research,* New York: Krieger, 1966.

11

TRANSRACIAL ADOPTIONS: CAN WHITE PARENTS BRING UP A HEALTHY BLACK CHILD?

By

Joyce A. Ladner

Although transracial adoptive placements have been made since the late 1940's, it was not until 1972 at the third annual meeting of the National Association of Black Social Workers that strong opposition to this practice was launched. The black social workers passed a resolution which stated that, "Black children should be placed only with Black families whether in foster care or for adoption. Black children belong physically, psychologically and culturally in Black families in order that they receive the total sense of themselves and develop a sound projection of the future." (Position Statement on Transracial Adoptions by NABSW Task Force, September, 1972, mimeograph.) Reporting on this controversial resolution the New York Times wrote on April 8, 1972:

> Adoption of black children by white families...were termed "a diabolical trick" by Audrey Russel of Philadelphia. She said, "Black children belong with black folk. This is a lethal incursion on the black family, just weakening us. It needs to be stopped."

Other blacks, including the press, professionals and laymen debated the question, "can white parents raise healthy black children? Can they provide them with the necessary black identity?"

The advocates of transracial adoption took a vigorous stand in defending their views and actions, and in redefining their original commitment. It must be noted that there are a variety of positions taken in behalf of transracial adoptions. Not all of its supporters, as will be shown, believe that this is the most viable alternative to solving the problem of finding permanent homes for black children. Likewise all do not support the view that "any home is better than no home." Indeed, some of those who have adopted transracially now question the wisdom of having done so.

I will examine the responses and counter charges that proponents of transracial adoption have made to the black social workers' opposition. These are as follows:
(1) the formation of human identity is as important, and some believe moreso, as black identity; (2) transracial adoptions promote the concept of an integrated society, and may, in the long run have an impact on countering racial strife; (3) the NABSW's position reflects reverse racism and ideological concerns, rather than concern with children, and; (4) transracial adoptions have occurred in such large numbers because blacks do not adopt black children in sufficient numbers.

BACKGROUND

Transracial adoptions grew out of the concern of white families to find homes for the large numbers of black children in foster and institutional care. Black children have been traditionally classified as "hard to place," in much the same sense as the older white child, and the child with medical disabilities. In 1948, a black social worker in Minneapolis named Laura Gaskins placed a black child with a white family. In recalling this experience, she told me in an interview that at the time she made the placement, the black population in Minneapolis-St. Paul was extremely small. After being unable to locate a suitable black home for this child who had been in a succession of many foster homes in his first months, she was determined that his next home would be a permanent one. When a white couple indicated that they would not mind adopting the child, he was placed with them. The social worker, who came to Minnesota from a southern border state, made this placement with a family who resided in a rural area. It must be emphasized that this was not the beginning of an official agency policy on transracial adoption, but merely an isolated occurrence.

The first organized attempt by whites to find homes for black children was initiated in 1955 by the Minority Adoption

Recruitment of Children's Homes (MARCH), a federation of public and private agencies in the San Francisco Bay Area. MARCH recruited homes for children of Mexican-American, Negro, Italian, and to a lesser degree, children of European minority descent. Although its objective was to find homes for these children which would be compatible with their racial and ethnic backgrounds, a small number of the black children were adopted by blacks, according to a 1959 study by MARCH.

The Parents to Adopt Minority Youngsters (PAMY) was organized in 1957 in Minnesota. Harriet Fricke, a social worker, was the coordinator of the project whose aims were "to publicize the need for adoptive homes for minority race children and act as a referral center for people interested in adopting these children." *(PAMY's Progress)*. The project was sponsored by all the adoption agencies in the state as well as a number of other interested welfare organizations, and was administered by the Minnesota Department of Public Welfare. The objective of PAMY was to find homes for Indian, Mexican and Negro children, with the latter constituting the largest group. The original intention of PAMY was to find black homes for black children but requests about Negro children did come from white families and at least twenty minority children were placed in white families during the two years of PAMY's existence.

The first chapter of the Open Door Society in North America was organized in Montreal in 1959 by three white couples who had adopted mixed race children. These parents came together because of their concern for the large number of black and mixed race children who did not have permanent homes. According to a report on their experience by Margaret Edgar, the Montreal ODS worked closely with the Adoption Department of the Children's Service Center of Montreal to assist them in finding permanent homes. Only four years after the ODS was formed, they claimed great success. In the 1963 publication by the Montreal ODS under the editorship of Edgar, they state:

> As a result of the combined efforts of this voluntary organization, the Open Door Society, and the professional adoption agency, 201 children of mixed and minority racial background, mostly Negro and part Negro, have been placed with adoptive families during the last six years. Ninety-five percent of these families are of a different racial

background from their adopted children; this has meant the creation, by adoption, of inter-racial families. (p. 1)

This parent group served as a model for the formation of similar ones throughout North America, Europe and one affiliate in Australia. There are basically two such groups in the United States, the Open Door Society (ODS) and the Council on Adoptable Children (COAC). There have been three international conferences on transracial adoptions since 1969.

It is important to observe that over the years, the objectives of the ODS and COAC have been modified. While the Montreal ODS started with the objective of finding permanent homes for minority group children, and fully subscribed to the recruitment of white homes, they are now vitally concerned, as are many other affiliate groups, with recruiting black homes as well. They also express a great concern for the black social workers' position, and have organized ongoing programs in black culture and awareness for their black children.

One of the pioneers in the Canadian ODS movement is Margaret Edgar, who has adopted six children, 2 of whom are black. A social worker herself, she frequently speaks and writes about the Canadian transracial adoption experience. A reflection of the current Montreal ODS position was stated by Edgar recently and reported in the *Washington Post* of December 10, 1972. She said that "White families who adopt black children must make up their minds that they must become part of the black community and be black." She views transracial adoption as a less desirable alternative when it is impossible to find suitable black homes for black children. She also speaks harshly against those whites who would use such adoptions to express their liberalism. "You have to watch for those whites who want to raise a 'little white child in a brown skin.' This a naive concept. The world isn't made like that."

It is only natural that COAC and ODS groups would reflect different levels of awareness and sensitivity to the black social workers' concerns, but many have responded by modifying their programs. Most such groups now stress the adoption of other "hard to place" children especially older children of all races, and the handicapped.

The most critical issue articulated by the black workers is the development of black identity. In the following section I will analyze the counter position of the supporters of transracial adoption.

IDENTITY

Obviously the serious difficulty with assessing the degree to which transracially adopted children are able to develop a healthy identity has to do with the fact that the majority of those who have been adopted are still too young to make such a judgement possible. One of the ways the problem of identity has been approached is through studying the parents who adopted across racial lines.

There have been few studies conducted on the attitudes of these parents regarding the racial identification of their children. In 1965, Suzuki and Horn report that, in a study of 15 families who adopted transracially in the Los Angeles area in the early 1960's, "seven families stated frankly that they would tell their children about their backgrounds (and)..six families indicated that they did not know to what extent they would share the information about the children's racial backgrounds....The majority of these families had Caucasian-appearing children." Some of these parents had requested a child who, although transracial, was not visibly Negro.

Simon, in a 1973 study of 204 parents in Michigan, Missouri, Wisconsin and Minnesota, who had adopted transracially, found that "while only 5 percent of the parents who adopted Negro children and 11 percent of those who adopted Indian or Korean children currently perceive those children as White; 27 and 39 percent, respectively, expect that those same children eventually will identify themselves as White." However, Simon reports that fifty percent said that, as a result of the transracial adoption, their families are now "mixed;" 30 percent said they consider their family white, and the remaining 20 percent said that their family identified with the "human" race; a few said with "no race."

In a longitudinal study of 97 families residing in 15 states who adopted Indian children, Fanshel found that "the Indian child was not always viewed in the same manner as children of other minority groups..Many adoptive parents indicated they could not have taken Negro children." Fanshel, who conducted his study from 1958 to 1967 cautions that this be viewed as only one form of transracial adoption. On the matter of identity, he states:

> While most of the parents did not specifically seek out an Indian child for adoption--only one in five reported doing so-- the overall impression is that they not only became quite comfortable with the Indian characteristics of their children, but for most of the parents this took on a quite positive quality...Many of the families began to take on a strong, positive interest in the Indian background of their children and planned to encourage their children's interest in their own backgrounds.

In a recent exploratory study (1972), Edgar interviewed 6 of the transracially adopted individuals in Montreal who had reached adolescence and young adulthood. One was adopted in infancy, and the others were adopted as small children. She also studied a group of five foster children, four of whom were in white homes. She found that the foster children had particularly acute problems related to race. The adopted children had more ego strength and were generally more secure in dealing with racial problems than the foster children, a factor she attributed to their more secure home environment. All of these older children however, had experienced some form of discrimination, especially in dating. Edgar stated that when whites initially began adopting transracially in Montreal, "we were thinking only in terms of bringing up a child, children we cherished and loved. ...And it wasn't until they were in school that we realized that they had problems... problems for which we had not been prepared, ...of which we had no knowledge and with which we could not deal." In a speech presented to the Washington, D.C. Council on Adoptable Children Chapter in November, 1972, Edgar observed:

> By 1965 our children were beginning to enter school, and by 1967 we knew they were in trouble. Most of the children who were in school at the time . . . our bright children who had done very well at home, suddenly began to do not quite so well at school. They had problems with friends, some of them didn't seem to be quite so clever in the teachers' estimation as we had thought them; and we began to realize that there were some problems we were facing with them

and that they were facing that had to be coped with. That is when we began to look at our responsibilities as parents. ...

Edgar regards this as the turning point for the Montreal ODS, the point when they decided that they must develop a liaison with the black community,..."and to learn to be black."

There is an even greater scarcity of studies conducted with the children themselves. Simon's 1973 work on racial awareness examines color preference in adopted children. In a replication of the Clark and Clark doll study with 199 adopted white, black, American Indian and Asian children, and 167 natural children, Simon found that:

> ...Negro children who are reared in the special setting of multi-racial families do not acquire the ambivalence toward their own race that has been reported among all other groups of young Negro children. Our results also show that White children do not prefer "White" to other groups, and that there are no significant differences in the racial attitudes of any of the categories of children. (p. 20)

Some of the advocates of transracial adoption feel that the most important facet of the child's psychosocial development is his ability to view himself as a strong, secure and confident *human being*. This, they stress, is secondary to an awareness of himself as a *black* (or whatever the racial background) person. There are, of course, exceptions. A few parents whom I interviewed indicate that *black identity* is more important than any considerations of the universal assumption that "all people are the same." I will examine their "minority viewpoint" below.

A chief spokesman for the concept of "human identity" is Clayton Hagen, a Minnesota adoption worker. Hagen, who has long advocated transracial adoption, asserts that "identity is not necessarily fixed." ("Placement of the Minority Race Child," p. 32) He advocates that individuals should transcend the boundaries erected around them--boundaries which emanate from their various primary group memberships. Hagen asserts that:

> By thinking through how they see themselves, people are able to separate themselves from their race or their own nationality group and see themselves as human beings and therefore see other people as human beings. One's own or another's race is secondary. Those who are not able to

do this cannot of course be regarded as wrong because they see themselves as they feel their culture has regarded them, primarily in terms of race. ...A person who cannot find his identity in his humanness cannot then consider being parents to another human who may be of another race. (p. 32)

In the case of adoption, Hagen maintains that a parent's function is "to help a child of another racial background than one's own develop a concept of one's self as a worthwhile person..." He believes that, "if a child has a good feeling of self worth, the child can then deal with the many problems he may have to face and with which we are uncertain we can help him." (Hagen, p. 32)

Transracially adoptive parents who stress the importance of "human identity" emphasize racial equality, international understanding and cooperation, and the necessity for acceptance of people different from oneself on an "individual" basis. They dislike categorizations, stereotypes, and other concepts which negate understanding people as individuals. They insist that the most important resources parents can transmit to their children, adopted or natural, are security, love, warmth, affection, and a stable home atmosphere. These parents tend to emphasize that "a child is a child," and they feel there are basic problems in child-rearing which transcend racial and social class boundaries. Moreover, there are peculiar problems that they and their children face that are related to *adoption*. All adopted children, (if they are aware of having been adopted) must face a complex set of questions and problems related to having had two separate sets of parents, the biological and sociological. In addition to having to help the child to resolve his identity within the framework of being adopted, the transracially adoptive parent must also deal with the factor of race.

There are mixed responses to these two problems. Some transracially adoptive parents maintain that the most important issue they must resolve is that of the adoption itself. Being of another race is a secondary matter. As one parent exclaimed, "If I can get it over to my son that I love him in spite of his questions about who his real mother was and why she didn't keep him, I am sure I can get past the hurdle of race."

The transracially adoptive parent and child do not have to engage in the dilemma over whether the child is to be told of his birth status. It is a foregone conclusion that, because of the differences in racial background, he will automatically know. Some tend to feel that the transracially adopted child is less likely to encounter trauma or an identity "crisis" because of these observable differences. For example, Charles Olds, a social worker and a pioneer in these placements, said in an interview for this study:

> In a way it is easier for the adopted child who is black in a white family to resolve this identity, than it would be for the child who is in the family where he appears to be physically the same as his parents, and they have deluded him to think he is a part of the family when biologically, he wasn't.

Of course, one assumes that such a child will be adopted by parents who are committed to viewing him as *different*, but nevertheless, *valuable*. Unless his parents are able to view him in this manner, he will probably be reared as a "white child," and it is possible that his parents might make allowances and excuses for his color, hair texture, etc., if they do not have a healthy acceptance of the differences. Authorities on transracial adoption feel it absolutely necessary that the adoptive parents are able to understand, appreciate and bear the consequences of racial and cultural differences.

Many adoptive parents engage in denial, by telling the child that color does not make a difference, and that all "human beings" are the same. While the parents might feel this way, they cannot afford to make the assumption that the same holds true for those people on the outside with whom their child will eventually interact. In the long run, this denial will foster an unhealthy emotional attitude and negative self-image in the child, as indicated by Lawrence A. Scyner, a member of the Montreal Open Door Society, in a speech before the Second International Conference on Transracial Adoption held in Boston in 1970. In dealing with the topic "Looking Ahead to Youth and Adulthood," he said:

> Our experience has been that almost every child at some period of his life and into his adolescence has denied that he was black, has found himself hating or being afraid of black people. ... If the question of identification is not worked through, then this uncertainty shows up in denial, ...or just as often, in the child's self-image, or lack of self-esteem.

Another group of transracial adoption supporters, primarily those who have adopted, maintain that both black identity and a secure "human" identity are essential to the child's well-being. This group appears to be comprised of those parents who are socially conscious, most of them express some sympathy toward the black social workers' position. They are quite likely associated with COAC or ODS, and will frequently be found to engage in various types of "black enrichment" programs. In addition, they usually keep abreast of current trends in "Black America" and attempt to transmit black culture to the child through black literature, films, cultural shows, foods, etc. Many live in integrated communities and some have a few black friends with whom they are in close contact. However, I have found that these parents are more likely to try to relate black culture to the child on the intellectual level, (books, etc.) instead of the personal level (close black friends, etc.)

It is not uncommon to discover that some of the adoptive parents have *no* close black friends, and that they live in segregated white suburbia.

An interesting characteristic of this type of family is that they perceive themselves to be an "integrated" family instead of a white one. They remark that their entire family has changed as a result of the adoption, and that their white children and they themselves have profited greatly from the adoption. Without the experience that transracial adoption offers, their children would know less (and often very little) about black culture. This, they feel, is highly valuable to them, and in the long run, will enable a future generation of individuals to be more broadminded in understanding and adapting to racial and ethnic differences.

Many of these parents feel that they have developed more social consciousness since the adoption. Naive about race relations, they were too optimistic about the road ahead. They simply believed that their love for the child would be sufficient to enable them to solve the problems which might arise. Not all of them expected great difficulties. However, once the adoption was formalized, they began to encounter problems with relatives, especially grandparents, friends, and hostile strangers. Many of these parents said they were shocked when first confronted with hostile stares, parental rejection, dismay from their siblings and friends, and some occasional anonymous hostile remarks and threats. Another source of irritation was the overfriendliness toward the adopted child, which is viewed as a form of reverse discrimination. Although initial rejection of the adopted grandchild is frequent, this behavior is usually modified and the grandparent eventually accepts the child. For some grandparents, acceptance is total. For others it is not. Only in rare cases do the grandparents refuse ever to accept the child.

The abovementioned factors contribute to the increased awareness that these parents have experienced. As a result, they often find themselves attempting to establish closer relationships with blacks, and more openly trying to transmit to the child a healthy understanding and acceptance of his differences. Moreover, they also say that they are more honest and open with their own racial attitudes. The Montreal Open Door Society shows such an evolution in their philosophy and approach, as seen in a statement they adopted in 1971, published in their newsletter:

> Through increasing contacts with the black community and with the help of parents who have older (black) children we learned that love in our homes, although it is a most important factor, is not enough to successfully raise our multiracial children. For although we believe in the equality of races, the fact that we must face is that the society to which we belong does not. Our children must be made proud of their racial heritage and able to understand that the hostility or overfriendliness they meet are directed to them not as individuals but as people of their color. Each family must, in the manner most comfortable to it, deal with these facts so that their children will mature as adult human beings.

There are various levels of awareness among those who feel the importance of transmitting black identity to their adoptive children. As I mentioned in the foregoing, some of these parents, perhaps the majority, still tend to intellectualize this process. However, there are a few who have gone much further by moving into the black community, working in black settings, and by becoming advocates of the right of blacks to adopt black children. These parents say that they would not adopt another black child, because they feel that black children belong in black families.

One of the parents who feels strongly about the necessity for a transracially adopted child to develop a black identity stated:

If my child (age 2) has a solid image and awareness of himself as a black human being, no amount of outside abuse can really get him off that ground. I am not and cannot be responsible for all the outside influences, negative and positive, on him. I can do a great deal to prepare him for what is on the inside of him as we are attempting to do that now. ...We have (attempted to do) that since we first adopted him. That is why he has a lot of black playmates that are from 1 to 10 years old, and we also have black adults who take care of him frequently. We feel that this is a beginning...

This parent, who lives in an all black community in a large southern city, and who is a social worker with black youth, spoke of the process of developing black identity.

...We will do whatever is possible for white people to... being white provides a great limitation. If it means Joey going to Africa and living for a few years, then he will be in Africa to live for a few years. His biggest barrier in developing a solid image of himself may be us. I have worked with black youths for many years and I know a lot of black parents who bring obstacles to their own children's being in love with the fact that they are black. They want their kids to be white and this is very damaging. I don't think that Joey will (find) that we want him to be white. We are not oriented in that direction. So how do you prepare a child for racism? I'd say (you should) prepare him on the inside. Part of my job and what I am about is to combat institutional racism wherever I can. At the school level we plan to have proper textbooks placed in the schools. At the level of employment, we spend a lot of time with the power structure attempting to deal with hiring practices and things of that nature. (Although) I am interested in the institutional level, when it comes right down to it, ...if a man is in love with himself, he will survive. If he doesn't, I don't think there is anything I can do.

This father represents a very small group of such parents. Indeed, his views might be considered radical or extreme by those who advocate "love" and "human identity" as the primary factors parents should be able to provide.

There is no resolution to the controversy over whether white parents can impart black identity. This exists for basically two reasons. First, very little is known about the specific psychosocial processes involved in the formation of ethnic and racial identity. Second, although various transracially adoptive parents are, through trial and error, making attempts at transmitting this identity, their children have not yet reached the critical age of adolescence where the identity crisis is most evident.

There are some blacks including social workers, psychiatrists and others who feel that it is possible for whites to transmit black identity. They feel that one's core identity finds its basis in a healthy home environment, and agree with James Comer, a black child psychiatrist, that it is determined in large part "by the way he is treated in early life." Comer maintains that all of the child's additional experiences are added to, and serve to expand, this basic early home life. Therefore, if a child is adopted into a family that provides a warm, secure, and honest home life, his opportunity for developing the ethnic identity will be all the easier. Another black psychiatrist, James L. Curtis, who has worked for more than twenty years in providing psychiatric consultation to adoption agencies, feels that transracial adoption "is an eminently healthy development as it has been demonstrated endlessly that similar racial-group membership alone cannot serve as a reliable guarantee of a successful marriage, family, or home." In a 1972 article appearing in *Encore Magazine,* Curtis expresses this position:

> Nothing could be more short-sighted than an arbitrary denial to a child of the experience of growing up in a family the child calls his own or the insensitive denial to prospective adoptive parents of the pleasure of being parents on the grounds that they were not of the 'right' race.

Individuals who feel that a black home is ideal, but a white home is preferable to foster care and institutionalization do not give a blanket endorsement to transracial adoption. Adoptive parents, they feel, should be mature, able to accept differences, sensitive to their own prejudices and racism, and willing to place their families in an arena wherein the contacts with other blacks will be maximized. They are wary of those whites who do not understand the importance, or have an interest in "becoming part of the black community." They also object to other whites who seem to be motivated by guilt, the population explosion, civil rights, and some other social issues. Such whites, they argue, are more interested in proving a point for themselves, and will use the child to do so, than in the welfare of an orphaned child.

A black social worker who has long been active in the Open Door Society said, in an interview with the writer, that "Some parents have come into our groups (ODS) who insist that...my child is a child and I don't want to bring him up as a black child or white child." His reply to such parents is that:

...At this point in our society there are different kinds of expectations or roles that a black man has to fulfill, and white men do not. Therefore, you have to help this child deal with what society places on him. It doesn't mean that he's going to be inferior or superior but they must recognize that there is a different kind of value placed on a black kid. This is a part of the whole identity thing that children go through. Families living in a totally white area, having no black friends and associates for the child..cannot give the child this identity. ...Yes, I think a white family can do this.

Of course, ultimately time will determine whether or not identity of one group can be transmitted by members of another racial or ethnic group. Such a time will be when these children are able to speak for themselves.

TRANSRACIAL ADOPTIONS PROMOTE INTEGRATED SOCIETY

Transracially adoptive parents have a strong commitment to the goals of an integrated society in which individuals are judged on their merit instead of being evaluated on their group membership. Their commitment is also to justice, equality, understanding and acceptance of all people without regard for their racial, cultural, religious or nationality backgrounds. In this sense, their lives are guided by a strong sense of purpose, and by living their commitments. As a group they are also idealistic, independent of the views of other family members, and family centered. In *Transracial Adoption,* Thomas Nutt and John Snyder state:

for the transracial adoptions, family formation is an international valuative act. Whether or not its ramifications are fully understood or consciously intended, a transracial adoption is a personal statement of a transracial adoptions' sense of what a society ought to be.

These white adoptive parents have a strong commitment to a value which is no longer adhered to by a significant segment of the black population. Their emphasis on universal brotherhood and acceptance of individual differences comes at a time in the social, political and cultural arena of this society when blacks are adhering to cultural pluralism and racial separatist ideologies. Such blacks tend to view individual whites as a collectivity, and to assign them the label of "racist." For one to have adopted a black child is insignificant to such blacks, since they impute a variety of sinister motives to these parents. They are accused of having adopted with the intention of destroying black culture, of seeking to weaken the black family, of projecting their psychological needs and fantasies onto black children, especially male children, and of "taking" black children away from the black community to brainwash them. Unfortunately, the white parents' intentions are not viewed in a positive way by blacks who have rendered their verdict long before meeting the parents. When face to face contact occurs, the opponents do not usually change their attitudes.

Because the two groups are operating at different levels of awareness, commitment, and ideological/philosophical persuasion, presently there is little ground for consensus. Whereas black social workers are emphasizing group solidarity, political *control* and a developing social consciousness among blacks, transracially adoptive families emphasize the family unit, and the necessity that it be allowed to develop and function to its fullest capacity. Hence, the white parents are more child-centered and maintain that the welfare of the child should be placed above all else. Nutt and Snyder found that

> Transracial adoptions...are...viewing the world as a place to be made humane. They have grown up in a world (of) power and control, and found lacking their application through the conventional institutions of society.

Of course, it is much easier to reject power and control if one has been exposed to them, or has been socialized in a culture where one had access. It is vastly different, however, if this access has been denied.

The most moving expression I heard during the course of

this study came from a father in Minnesota who said that adopting a black child had made him identify with other blacks so much that "whenever I see police brutality against blacks on television I want to strike out against whites and come to the defense of my son's people."

REVERSE RACISM OF BLACK SOCIAL WORKERS

One of the accusations made against the black social workers and other foes of transracial adoption is that they are racist. The supporters feel the social workers are anti-white, much too abstract and theoretical about racial matters, instead of focusing on the needs of individual children, and finally they accuse them of making a "political" statement. Some parents are embittered over the controversy the black social workers' position has aroused; they have been thrust in the midst of the controversy against their will, and forced to defend their actions. They had considered their adoption to be a personal statement of their commitment to better child welfare services, equality and an integrated society. They also felt it was a private family matter. When the social workers challenged their right to parent black children, and when their motives for having adopted were questioned by people who attacked them for their alleged racism--individuals with whom they had never had any contact--many retreated and then fought back. Had not their very behavior been sufficient proof that they were not racist, but that they believed in equality and a fair opportunity for blacks?

Another concern of the parents is that the problem these adoptions might cause for the child are greatly exaggerated by the black social workers. They feel that the level and breadth of the controversy is disproportionate to the actual numbers of children being adopted. The majority of the parents I interviewed did not feel that the adoptions pose any significant threat to the black family and black culture because of the very small numbers of children involved. As one parent remarked, "I just can't see transracial adoption in terms of a great cultural significance...I just see it has human interaction between a relatively limited number of people. And it sure doesn't pose a threat."

In addition to the question of numbers, there is also the

concern that the black social workers are arguing on a theoretical level, and that their position is based on political assumptions and concerns. The real problem for these parents is the individual child whose needs should be met by a set of permanent parents, regardless of whether they are black or white. They argue that it is an easy way out for black social workers to raise the political questions without following them up with the necessary action to insure more black adoptions. Black social workers have been accused of being too ego involved, and of having rendered an absurd position.

There is the persistent theme expressed among these parents that black critics aren't really concerned about the child. One parent remarked, "I think they should be more concerned with these little black babies rather than with their theories."

WHITE PARENTS BELIEVE BLACKS DO NOT ADOPT

The reason cited most frequently by parents for adopting transracially is that they wanted to provide homes for children who are least likely to be adopted. The adoption profession invented the term "hard to place" to describe black children, older white children, and the handicapped. There appears to be a genuine concern among transracially adoptive parents for the plight of the black, so-called "hard to place" child. Many of them had already adopted a white child, and a few had adopted Indian or Asian children. Moreover, some 80% of the parents in my study already had biological children before adopting transracially. Generally, they adhere to the "room for one more" concept, introduced by Harriet Fricke in the Minnesota PAMY project previously cited. She argued that the most valuable way they can carry out their commitment is through adopting a "hard to place" child.

There also exists the persistent notion that blacks do not adopt. Some parents feel that the reason for such a large number of so-called "hard to place" black children is because blacks, for a variety of reasons have not come forth to adopt.

One of the accusations whites and other advocates of transracial adoption have made against black social workers is that few of them have stepped forward to provide homes for these children. As one black student remarked, in a letter published in *Encore Magazine* in 1972, "I don't see many of these black social workers adopting black children. ...By the way,is Cenie Williams (national president of NABSW) adopting any children?"

This statement strikes to the crux of the controversy because it is difficult for critics to make their position legitimate without also working to insure that black homes are located for the waiting children. Otherwise their concerns are relegated to the level of rhetoric, and the other critical issues they raise are diminished in importance.

Although evidence collected by Robert Hill of the National Urban League, in a publication entitled *Strengths of Black Families,* indicates that large numbers of blacks do in fact adopt both formally and informally, many of the white parents who adopt black children continue to believe that blacks generally do not adopt.

Most parents have never had first hand experience with the traditions and customs of blacks and have therefore accepted the myths and misconceptions propogated by adoption and foster care organizations and by insensitive and uninformed policy makers. It is easy to understand why the myths are so widely embraced because the actual numbers of black adoptions do appear to be quite a bit lower than the comparative numbers of white adoptions.

There are several reasons for this. In a larger study, I discuss the role that adoption agencies have played in discouraging black adoptions. Adoption agencies seem to have found it much easier to make transracial placements than to aggressively recruit black adoptive families. When white parents began efforts to adopt black or mixed race children, it must have provided a temporary solution to the problem of an abundance of "hard to place" black children. It certainly made the jobs of agencies easier because they did not have to go to the trouble of setting up special recruitment programs aimed at a black clientele, nor hire a black social worker to assist in such a program. Moreover, these placements were made in the beginning with a minimum of planning. Inadequate screening of the parents, very few, and oftentimes, no supportive services (counseling, etc.), and almost no follow-up was characteristic of most of the early adoptions.

Only recently have adoption agencies begun to evaluate seriously the long range consequences of transracial placements, and to become more concerned with the characteristics and motivations of applicants. The agencies' policies did more to contribute to the misconceptions regarding blacks and adoption than to inform. Therefore, it is not surprising that a great many transracially adoptive parents were motivated by the need to provide homes for children whom they felt would be the least likely to be adopted. It is also probable that some parents approached the adoption with a "rescue fantasy."

One of the emerging concerns some express is the need to help to reform agency policy in order to make it less difficult for blacks to adopt. Open Door Society and Council On Adoptable Children groups throughout the country are becoming increasingly involved in lobbying for more adequate child welfare legislation such as adoption subsidies, and such court reforms are terminating parental rights in order to free the children for adoption. Some of the parents who adopted before becoming aware of the discriminatory roles of the agencies, are now involved in the reform efforts. Interestingly, as has been pointed out, some indicate that they now feel that black children belong in black homes, and would not adopt another black child because of their present awareness of the issues and problems involved. Accordingly they are also more accepting of the need for extra efforts to provide their black child with a balanced social environment in order that his ability to form a healthy black identity is maximized.

CONCLUSION

Transracial adoptions originally grew out of the concern to find homes for so-called "hard to place" (black) children. Agencies which had traditionally catered to a white middle class clientele entered this new arena of adoptions without undertaking the necessary planning. The immediate goal was to fulfill the requests of white middle class parents, while simultaneously envisioning some progress in solving one of their thorniest problems. It has been emphasized that perhaps most white adoptive parents lacked an awareness of the diverse problems, conflicts and complications that would eventually arise. Therefore, many were stunned by the controversy raised by the black social workers.

The black social workers were quite successful in causing agencies to re-examine their policies toward transracial adoptions and in forcing many of them to initiate, for the first time, programs directed toward increasing black adoptions. The social workers also forced many white parents to face certain critical issues affecting their black children. The end result has been a decrease in these adoptions. Between 1971 and 1972 there was an estimated 40% decrease thought to be caused largely by the black social workers' opposition. A survey conducted by the Opportunities Division of the Boys and Girls Society of Portland, Oregon has found a decline in transracial adoptions for each year since 1972.

Yet, transracial adoptions still pose a thorny problem because the issues have not really been resolved.

Although one might criticize agency policy, and the white parents, the most crucial issue is that homeless minority children have been adopted. At the same time, too few efforts have been made by the black middle class to adopt. Ultimately, the critics' concerns will not diminish until there is not only a continuing decrease in transracial adoptions, but a corresponding increase in black family adoptions.

SOURCES

Curtis, James L., "Point-Counterpoint: Should White Parents Adopt Black Children?" *Encore Magazine,* December 1972.

Edgar, Margaret (ed.), *Some Experiences in Inter-Racial Adoption by Members of the Open Door Society, Inc.,* Montreal, 1963.

Fanshel, David, *Far from the Reservation; The Transracial Adoption of American Indian Children,* New Jersey: The Scarecrow Press, Inc., 1972.

Falk, Lawrence, "Trans-Racial Adoption: A Comparative Study," Concordia College, Moorhead, Minnesota, 1968.

Fricke, Harriet, "Interracial Adoption: The Little Revolution," *Social Work,* July 1965.

Hagen, Clayton, "Placement of the Minority Race Child," Minneapolis Lutheran Family and Children Services (mimeographed.)

Hill, Robert B., *The Strengths of Black Families*, New York: Emerson Hall, 1972.

The MARCH Committee, "Adoptive Placement of Minority Group Children in the San Francisco Bay Area: A Study by MARCH," San Francisco, 1959.

National Association of Black Social Workers Task Force, "Position Statement on Transracial Adoptions," September 1972 (mimeographed.)

Nutt, Thomas E. and Snyder, John A., *Trans-Racial Adoption*, Cambridge: M.I.T. Press, 1972.

Open Door Society Bulletin, Montreal, Canada, September 1971.

Parents-to-Adopt-Minority Youngsters, "PAMY's Progress," A Report on Recruitment Campaign conducted by Parents-to-Adopt-Minority Youngsters, St. Paul, Minnesota Department of Public Welfare, 1963.

Raynor, Lois, *Adoption of Nonwhite Children: The Experience of the British Adoption Project*. London: Allyn and Unwin, Ltd., 1971.

Scyner, Lawrence A, "Looking Ahead to Youth and Adulthood," in *Children Who Wait*, Proceedings of the Second International Conference on Trans-racial Adoption, Boston, 1970.

Simon, Rita, "White Parents of Non-white Children: An Analysis of Transracial Adoption," University of Illinois, 1973, (mimeographed.)

_____ "An Assessment of Racial Awareness, Preference, And Self-Identity Among White and Adopted Non-White Children," University of Illinois, 1973.

St. Denis, Gerald, *Interracial Adoptions in Minnesota: Self Concept and Child Rearing Attitudes of Caucasian Parents Who Have Adopted Negro Children*, Unpublished doctoral dissertation, University of Minnesota, 1969.

Suzuki, Ryo and Horn, Marilyn, "Follow-up Study on Negro-White Adoptions," Department of Adoptions, Country of Los Angeles, 1965 (mimeographed.)

PERSONAL INTERVIEWS CITED IN TEXT

James Comer, Psychiatrist, November, 1973.

Laura Gaskins, Director of Adoption Division, Hennepin County Department of Public Welfare, Minneapolis, Minnesota, November, 1972.

Charles Olds, Director of Pierco-Warwicke Adoption Agency, Washington, D.C., March 1972

Adoptive Parents

12

A FRIENDSHIP: PART ONE

By

Gloria Feman Orenstein

There are many divisive forces in our society that mitigate against the chances of inter-racial friendships developing beyond the superficial level. It even amazes me today as I write this and meditate upon the forces in my background which were set in motion in order to prevent such a friendship from ever forming, that I feel compelled to acknowledge the fact that Adah Askew is one of my closest and most intimate friends, one whom I love very dearly.

There was an undeniable share of covert racism that could be uncovered in my background and there were several instances of overt prejudice which were certainly part of my early conditioning. Although nothing was ever mentioned openly about my family's feeling towards blacks, my family brought me up in a white middle-class suburb in Queens where I had little chance to meet or form a close friendship with a black person. (Sociologically, one could say that having been raised in all white neighborhoods and having attended all white schools for twenty-one years, the likelihood of my forming a profound and lasting relationship with a black person was small indeed.)

My first experience with racism came when I was about ten years old. A black family of some renown was about to purchase a house around the corner from ours, and I recall the hushed whispers every time I asked about who our new neighbors were to be. When my parents didn't want me to understand what was being said they reverted to the use of Yiddish, which was the language in which they discussed both sex and money. I never did learn Yiddish, but I understood the meaning of the word "schwartze," and I knew that a black family was to move into that house and that for some reason I was not permitted to overhear my parents' reaction to this highly charged subject. Later on I came to find out that they had felt that their property would be devalued if the family were to move in. The family never did move to our neighborhood; the hushed discussions were abandoned, and silence again prevailed on the subject of race relations.

I was born in 1938, lived in a predominantly Jewish neighborhood, and attended an elementary school that was 90% Jewish. Thus, I had not experienced much anti-Semitism, particularly since the public schools acknowledged Jewish holidays. Most of my friends and my parents' friends were Jewish.

This lack of knowledge and lack of awareness of my own ethnic stigma might have continued right on through college, had I not been rezoned for high school and obliged to attend Richmond Hill High School in Queens, rather than the largely Jewish Forest Hills or Jamaica High Schools. We were the first group of students who were rerouted from these schools to Richmond Hill, because the schools had become underpopulated. Although I traveled with Jewish friends from my neighborhood, I entered a world in which I was forced to realize abruptly that to be Jewish was to be part of an ethnic minority in the world at large. When, for example, I inquired about Brandeis University, I was advised to consult my Rabbi. I was constantly on display-- giving first-hand accounts of the celebration of Channukah, Passover, and other festivals--despite the fact that these were rarely observed in my home. Although I don't recall any overt discrimination on the part of the other students, I remember that I did feel excluded from the activities of some of my friends that revolved around their church affiliations. Many of the more interesting and intelligent students from the Richmond Hill area belonged to church groups, and socializing outside of school was difficult for these reasons. I had my own group of friends, largely Jewish, and we formed our own social circle.

It was only as I prepared to leave for college that I remember another incident involving racism. If I search my memory carefully for clues I recall another family discussion in Yiddish in which the subject "schwartzes" came up. My aunt was telling my mother that she hoped my education would not liberate me to the point of bringing home black friends from college. Looking back upon the conversation, it seems that this must have been a terribly threatening subject, for there was, indeed, little likelihood that I would meet any black students at Brandeis in 1955. At the time the remarks were made they were both disconcerting and alarming to me, largely because of the way in which they were whispered. I admit that I was probably less outraged by the racial prejudices of my family (I had a very low consciousness about these issues at the time), than I was frightened by what seemed to me to be yet another taboo. I was being conditioned to believe that there was something hushed and secret about inter-racial relationships. This, like sex and money was obviously another area to be carefully avoided with my parents. I knew that if I questioned them on these subjects I would be accused of harboring some evil thoughts, incriminated for breech of silence, or more precisely, for embarrassing them and exposing their concealed racist prejudices. It is clear that my fear dominated my curiosity. I had been a passive, obedient and submissive daughter. Little did I realize that this, too, was a calculated part of my conditioning.

As could have been predicted, all of my friends in college were white middle-class Jews. During my last year of college the civil rights movement was born, and my mind was suddenly opened to the vast farce that had been perpetrated upon me, to the horrors of racism that I had ignored, to the information I had been denied because of my privileged middle-class upbringing. I vowed that I would not raise my own children in just such a white ghetto.

However, throughout college my rebellion against this intellectually stifling middle-class background took the form of a denial of materialistic values and of the capitalistic mentality rather than that of a passion for social reform or political activism. I sought personal escape from the suburban life-style by marrying someone with whom I could affirm a quest for cultural enrichment and with whom I would transcend the materialism that my parents had embraced because of their own material deprivation.

My father had been raised on the lower East side in New York City, in a family of ten children. The great drama of his poverty and his struggle during the depression has left an indelible imprint upon me. I knew that to be a Jew looking for employment during the depression was a great hardship and affliction. Trained in both engineering and law, my father was not hired in either of these fields, due to discrimination. He ended up by becoming a teacher and then a businessman. My mother's family was also very poor. The lasting memory of both grandmothers that had been transmitted to me through my parents is one of their great fortitude coupled with their deep sadness. While I empathized with my parents' desire for material acquisitions, I also saw that these comforts did not necessarily bring about happiness. I felt that I wanted to seek meaning through more spiritual and intellectual values.

When I met Adah Askew (then known as Betty Bargonetti) I had been married to a French Jew for nine years, who had spent his childhood in hiding in France during the Second World War. This marriage speaks of my own psychic identification with the suffering of my people, for I had tremendous compassion for my husband's war-time experiences. This identification with the oppression of my own ethnic group helped prepare me to understand the oppression of black people. At that time I already had two young daughters. During the period of my life in which I came to know Adah my major battle was no longer waged against the materialistic values of my parents, but against the oppression of women in our society. I had been an honors student throughout my college career and had earned an M.A. at Radcliffe Graduate School. After the birth of my first child I suffered a tremendous postpartum depression and, on my own, reapplied to graduate school and taught French as a Graduate Assistant, which cured me of the depression--one that my psychiatrist had felt could only be treated adequately and overcome permanently by a rest cure. (He was astounded that added responsibilities and an additional commitment to extra work could enable me to put meaning back into my life and to recover.) I had put myself back together again, alone, and in the only way I knew how. But, in a pre-feminist era I was considered neurotic for my academic ambitions and for my aspirations to a career outside the home. However, I had persevered, and when I met Adah I was working on my doctorate in Comparative Literature at NYU. We had moved next door to each other in a Mitchell-Lama middle-income cooperative in Manhattan. Adah and I had come there from Queens for similar reasons--to escape from the middle-class suburban life-style. We had come to raise our children in the vital and integrated community of the Upper West Side.

Adah was in undergraduate school at night. She was exactly

my age, and was a French major who had just returned from France, where she had gone to affirm her own quest for autonomy and independence. She had turned to a foreign country for acceptance of her black identity, and when she returned from France she knew that Black was indeed Beautiful. We had our studies in common, our passionate search for excitement in common, our marriage and our children in common--and so much more.

My husband's work took us to Italy for a year and so the friendship with Adah, of only a few months' duration, had to be postponed until we returned. During my absence, our building had been divided politically over a school strike issue. I had missed that confrontation, and in fact, had always felt apologetic about the fact that we were sending our children to the French Lycee instead of to the public schools. Both my husband and I, for our own reasons, wanted our children to be bilingual. This rationale usually exempted us from the heated debates on the issues of public versus private-education and the tendency for white middle-class families to desert the public schools.

Adah and I generally did not discuss these incendiary topics. We often spent weekend evenings socializing at Adah's apartment or at mine, and it seems, as I look back upon it now, that we were united by the fact that we were both put down by our husbands for our vitality, our energy, our interests, our love of eccentric people, our emotionality, and for our ability to talk endlessly on the phone. We shared a mutual conflict. We were managing to do double jobs--to keep the home and to pursue our educational objectives. Yet, because of financial dependence upon our husbands, we were forced to submit to ridicule for our strength, our enthusiasm, our excitement--for all those qualities that had been instrumental in our personal survival.

I admired Adah for what seemed to me to be her superior ability to endure hardship with complaining, for her capacity to struggle against all the odds that opposed her in order to affirm her own integrity. Having married young and been denied a college education, here she was the mother of two children, still commuting nights to Hunter College for her undergraduate degree, much as I had commuted to NYU for my own graduate degree. I admired her perseverance, her pride, her talent. She found me to be a complainer (in the tradition of my two grandmothers). I had been handed everything on a silver platter and still complained if we could not afford some extra luxury. I wanted to afford private schools for the children, music and art lessons, trips abroad, graduate school, nursery school, sitters, books, concerts, theater tickets, and all the extras that squeeze the budget of a college professor to the breaking point. I was a Jewish American Princess in a certain sense. I didn't want cars, furs or jewels, but I wanted all the intellectual and cultural luxuries. Adah looked down upon my ignorance of poverty, of hardship, of struggle, in the same way that my parents did. Strangely enough though, none of these possible points of conflict separated us or caused a rift to come between us in our friendship.

Adah was my friend because we shared the same dream--the dream of a time when all races would come to live in harmony, the dream of a time when there would be no more oppression between male and female, the dream of a time when we would emerge and fulfill all that potential that had been repressed for so many years, and when we would pursue our chosen careers without being made to feel guilty for wanting to step outside the appointed roles that society had prescribed for men, women, blacks, or Jews.

When we met we were in equal financial and social postions. We both had apartments in the Upper West Side, marriages that in our eyes were less than perfect, but we supposed, could have been much worse, and two intelligent children. But we both had something that our husbands seemed to lack, and that, it appeared to us, most of our neighbors also lacked--a sense of adventure.

If I had to pinpoint one thing that attracted me to Adah, it was the fact that she had taken off for Paris alone one summer in defiance of all conventions, in order to fulfill her lifetime dream of adventure and independence. Though she paid heavily for it in her marital relationship, she was proud to have done it, and used to say that she would do it again if she had her life to live over. My own turn for adventure came a few years later when, having written my dissertation, I came to meet several of the artists and writers whose work I had studied. I followed one artist in particular to both France and Mexico, because I knew that this was an important form of intellectual adventure.

Rather than berate each other for political intrigues that,

I suppose, we could have thrown in each other's faces daily, we supported each other in our mutual and separate struggle to emerge from our private oppression and to transcend the sordidness of social discrimination in a self-affirmative direction.

I suppose that when I analyze it now I see that we both had a great talent and capacity for alchemy, for transforming the suffering of the struggle into a positive joy through the ceaseless energy we put into our work and through our love of people. Adah's friends and my friends would not always have liked each other, but we two could accept each other's tastes and choices despite the criticism we received. Adah went through a period in which she was much berated for having white friends. I understood that I was implicated in this conflict as much as her white husband must have been. I felt vibrations of distrust and hostility. She would ask me repeatedly which side I would choose when fighting broke out in the streets. She wanted to know if she could trust my loyalty to her and to the blacks no matter what might occur. When she affirmed her African heritage by getting an Afro and going into African dance with Pearl Primus, I supported her because she was a talented dancer, and I felt that we should be recognized for our talents and our obsessions. Similary I had asked for approval of my own choice of Surrealism as a topic for my dissertation. Both choices appeared equally absurd to our husbands. I supported her search for the ancient source of her heritage, and for knowledge of her racial and ethnic roots. Had I not done precisely the same thing when I enrolled in the Slavic Studies program at Radcliffe in order to learn about my own Russian ancestry? I was proud of her and of her defiance of all conventional choices. Here was a woman who could be a terrific cook, who could keep an immaculate house, and who could study all night without complaining, who could participate in an African Dance Program at the United Nations, who could entertain friends without tiring, and without ever giving in to those feelings of self-pity to which I all too frequently succumbed. Here was a woman who had been refused rides by white cab drivers, who had had stones thrown in her window when she moved into her apartment in Queens, who was questioned on all credit cards because of her white Italian surname, but who would recover and assert herself even more proudly and more defiantly the next time. She seemed to surpass me in energy, in *joie de vivre*, in confidence, in worldly experience, and in faith in the woman's power and ability to make it independently in a white man's world. Here was a woman that no oppressive force could vanquish. She transmuted the pain of suffering into the power of affirmation. She was as fascinating, intelligent, sensitive and dynamic as anyone I had ever known. She could mingle with those from the streets as easily as she could converse with her friends from the university. And she never chose to eliminate one group or the other from her life. She was truly multi-dimensional.

In the early days of our friendship she was more brittle, or as she prefers to say, she "had rough, hard edges." She had less patience for my self-indulged wallowing in feminist complaints. She had come from a lineage of proud people whose women had always worked. In the face of racial oppression, the oppression of women seemed something rather trivial to her. The greater social sin was the treatment of blacks. I empathized with her, yet I maintained that she did not sympathize with my feelings which were valid for my own personal experience. This was her hard edge. She was judgemental. Those who were not raised on the streets did not deserve to complain.

A transformation has overcome Adah since she entered a graduate program in counseling. Group work, Arica training, and counseling experience have made her empathetic to an extreme, sensitive beyond the demands of professionalism. All of her past hurts and defenses seem to have been exorcised. She has literally transmuted that anger into love, alchemized that energy of pain into a dedication to others, to healing them and to helping them seek a positive solution to their problems. Her "commitment" to this profession can only be described as a "mission."

Adah has, and has always had, the gift of love, and love is probably found as rarely in one race as in another. There are very few human beings that can take the risk of loving beyond color and racial boundaries. But Adah has taken all those risks. There is no boundary, whether racial, ethnic or linguistic that can block her desire to reach out to others.

In a year when I was involved with seperating from my husband after a 16 year marriage, Adah was the person to whom I turned on a daily basis in order to learn to survive. Despite the invaluable emotional support of others, she seemed to possess that unique knowledge of how to overcome humiliation and rejection, for that very struggle had been a part of her everyday life experience. She knew that those who do the rejecting and the wounding have no innate superiority. Whereas the others who have helped me could lecture to me about the need to transform my anger and my panic into life-affirming energies, Adah had shown me how this was done, for it was what she had been doing all her life.

Here is a concrete example of the kind of thing I have learned from Adah. Two summers ago we decided to learn to play tennis, each for our own personal reasons. I was using my last resources of strength to try to rescue a dying marriage. My husband had turned to sports with a passion, and since I was too frightened to learn to ski, I intended to give tennis one desperate and last all-out effort. My determination was only matched by my sense of inferiority in physical ability. I had tried to play tennis many times over the past years, and I only had memories of sweating in the hot sun and chasing balls that were lost in the grass. I knew before I began that this attempt was also doomed to failure.

When we began to play Adah would appear at my door each morning bright and early, looking cheerful and enthusiastic, and raring to go in her new white tennis outfit. I wore old plaid shorts, green sneakers--whatever I could dig up, because I would never have invested in a tennis outfit that I knew would go to waste. I was defeated before I had even begun. We would ride over to Central Park on our bikes and reserve a court. Then we would return at the appointed hour and get down to chasing balls in the hot sun. I assumed that if Adah had gone to the trouble of buying a tennis outfit she must have known that she would be good at the game. When we got on the courts I realized that we were both beginners, that she was on my level, and I wondered how she could remain so cheerful throughout these discouraging hot hours on the court. Yet each time one hour was up, she left the court elated, excited and eager to return the next day. I thought that she must be insane. I was depressed. I would give up. She insisted: "Glo, you're not giving yourself half a chance." She only managed to convince me to return because I knew that I had to understand her bizarre and aberrant form of logic. How could she repeat defeat daily and not be discouraged? We went back every day. We asked people to help us with our volley. We learned to socialize with those who played better than we did and who could help us to improve our stroke.

By the end of the summer we had actually learned to sustain long volleys on the court, and I had come to enjoy the sense of accomplishment, the exercise, the challenge and the energy of the exchange. But more importantly--I learned a valuable lesson. Adah's strength was not a physical strength but a strength of the will. She knew that talents were not god-given, but man-made. I will never forget my tennis lessons. They were some of my most precious lessons in life. Adah dressed the part, for she knew that one's self-image is enhanced if one can imagine oneself in the role in advance. Half of the battle is already won if we can believe ourselves equal to the task. When my own marriage did fail, despite the tennis lessons, I was to apply Adah's philosophy to the other areas of my life. I have learned not to honor my defeatist tendencies and to focus upon my energy, upon my potential for growth and for transcendence.

It had always been a common source of humor in both houses that I was studying the occult in art and literature. Adah had recognized her own affinity for such areas of investigation, but I felt that both she and her husband always looked upon my love of Surrealism and the occult as one of my own peculiar eccentricities. Nothing could have surprised me more when I returned to New York one recent summer than to find Adah meditating daily and involved in the Arica training program. What astonished me however, was her accomplishment in the area in which I had specialized, but in such a purely intellectual way. I would write about psychic powers; she would develop them. She has now instructed me in meditation as well, and I realize that we have reached a point of absolute parity in our relationship in terms of interests. Adah progresses by quantum leaps. Her ability to enter new fields, to master new skills, to seek out new self-transforming experiences, to face herself, coupled with the pace of her intellectual growth and emotional maturity never ceases to amaze me. As I write this she is going through turmoil of her own marital separation, and once again we have grown closer together in the sharing of our deepest conflicts.

Yet we are very similar despite our different modes of relating to the world. If my struggles are transmuted into words rather than acts, we still share the same dream and we speak from the same pain. If I am more academic in the application of my education and she is more pragmatic, we are both, nevertheless, teachers, but of different kinds of knowledge. We have both been self-sacrificing in our marriages and in our lives. We have both been hurt by the inability of others to appreciate our giving and our sharing. Yet we have never been crippled by that denial of praise. We have only become more determined than ever to validate those energies in others whom we see being discredited, discriminated against, and put down in the same ways we were.

This article was not programmed into the original scenario of my life as it was written by my parents. Fortunately the creative spirit and the humanitarian impulse can transcend even the most rigid forms of social conditioning. But we also learn bitter lessons from the past. I have learned that the personal solution to social injustice, although it may provide a beautiful example of the triumph of individual freedom, is, in the long run, no guarantee that humanitarian values will prevail. In recent years I have become more socially and politically active. Most of my energy has been channeled into the Feminist Movement. In order to bring about effective change the personal solution must be wedded to collective action. Only when these changes have occurred will our task as citizens of this planet be accomplished.

I have been a student of Surrealism for some time now, and the triple aspirations of the Surrealist Movement are those which I personally embrace. They include the desire to change life, to transform the world, and to remake from scratch human understanding. Until we make this dream a reality we must continue to struggle for equality and freedom. If in some small way my friendship with Adah Askew has served this ideal then it will have achieved even more than it has already given me in terms of a profoundly meaningful personal relationship. It will show that love is an active force in the world and that its power transcends any barrier ever invented by man throughout the history of civilization.

A FRIENDSHIP: PART TWO

By

Adah Askew

I've lived next door to Gloria for the past nine years and as time has passed our friendship has grown. The intensity of our relationship amazes many people. Perhaps it's because I'm black and Gloria is white that our closeness surprises folks. Well, at times it astounds me too, but not for the same reason. Color has never been a factor in determining my choice of friends. I usually base my selection on what and how much we have in common. When Gloria and I first met I really didn't think we had any points of reference which could bring us together. The only interest we seemed to share was a deep concern for how our children would ultimately spend their summer of 1966 (we were both new to the Upper West Side and, with summer fast approaching, we needed to find a day camp that was reasonably priced and easily accessible). The difference in my background and Gloria's made it difficult for me to conceive of us having any meaningful common focus, other than our children, which would bring us together.

Gloria spent her formative years and her adolescence growing up in an all-white middle-class suburb in Queens. I spent my formative years in much the same way: I lived in a middle-class white suburb in New Jersey. My adolescent years, however, were spent growing up in Harlem. At the time when Gloria and I met I was focused on my Harlem experience and was flatly denying any affiliation with my middle-class past. Having recently moved from Jackson Heights, Queens probably contributed to my attitude. The various negative experiences which had permeated my existence while I lived there had left me bitter and suspicious of all white people. The development in which I lived had been 99% white middle-class and most of my neighbors were Jewish.

Some of them were nice, but others refused to speak simply because I was black. Others found my blackness so offensive to them that they refused to even ride in the same elevator with me. I realize, in retrospect, that since Gloria was a white middle-class Jew I was forcing her to atone for the sins of a group of people whom she neither knew nor resembled in the least. My behavior toward her was cordial but distant. I had moved to the Upper West Side, a thoroughly integrated neighborhood precisely to avoid being "different." This being the case, I wasn't about to establish a friendship with someone who I felt would put me right back into the same type of space out of which I had just moved.

Part of my reticence to establish communication with Gloria was her seeming innocence about what was going on in what I considered to be "my world." After all, what could she possibly know about life? More importantly, what could she know about suffering or how it felt to be rejected by both her people as well as my own? I never imagined that she would be capable of understanding anything at all about me. I think I actually believed that having been born and raised a middle-class Jew gave Gloria immunity to all of the pain which was so much a part of my day-to-day experience. And in addition, she neither "pop her fingers" nor "hang." Initially, I couldn't honestly see myself relating to someone who knew absolutely nothing about the "struggle" or the street. It's not clear to me even now precisely what events took place that caused me to change my attitude towards Gloria, but eventually it did soften.

Maybe the friendship which developed between our children created the context for us to get to know one another just as people. When that began to happen I felt more comfortable and was able to let down some of my defenses. At this point we were able to establish a dialogue. The more time Gloria and I spent together the more evident it became that she and I were not so unalike at all. Actually we had quite a lot in common. Just for starters, we were both involved in caring for our families during the day while attending school at night. Although our educational pursuits were on different levels. (Gloria was a Ph.D candidate at New York University and I was a B.A. candidate at Hunter College) our level of commitment and anxiety was the same. Further, we had a mutual interest in France, its literature, its language, its culture and its people. I took a personal interest in the African countries and various islands in the West Indies which had formerly been French colonies. Gloria's field of comparative literature had drawn her to the works of writers who came from some of these areas. I was a French major so my "French connection" with Gloria was a really bright spot in our relationship. She was a tremendous help to me. Fluent in the language, she often proofread my term papers which were written in French and she was always supportive and full of encouragement whenever I felt that French was going to "do me in."

Another extremely important common denominator for us was our less-than-satisfactory marriages. Although neither of us was willing, initially, to admit it to the other, we both wanted out of what was supposed to be a life-time commitment. But because both of us had married when we were quite young (Gloria at the age of 20 and I at 18) we found it hard to believe we could actually make it on our own without a man. We felt too inadequate to even try, so we developed staying power, and acted the part of dutiful wives. We even went so far as to pretend to be happy. Once we discovered that we were both role-playing it became easier, for a while, for each of us to keep up our act.

As Gloria and I got to know each other better we began to socialize as a foursome. This was when we discovered one more common bond. Both our husbands had keen minds, sharp tongues, were athletic and took great pleasure in playing the game of "put your wife down in the presence of others." No doubt our exuberance and our restless desire to become a part of what was happening in the universe outside of our homes was indeed partly responsible for the way our husbands reacted toward us. So, maintaining a degree of harmony within our family structures while attempting to live, instead of merely survive, was a serious problem for the two of us. Both men came from European backgrounds. This was decidedly not in our favor. Early conditioning would not permit either of them to comfortably support our efforts to become more assertive. Women had their place and we were rapidly making strides to move out of the one to which we had been ascribed. Gloria's husband was a Frenchman and mine was a first generation Italian-American who might just as well have been born in Sicily. Their responses to our desire for a degree of freedom were usually negative and hostile. They both viewed our modes of self-expression as our means of copping out of the housewife role. (African Heritage dance was my outlet, surrealism was Gloria's.) It's no surprise that Gloria and I are now both divorced.

The process of arranging our difficult divorces was tension-producing for us both, often giving cause for self-doubt. But Gloria has managed beautifully, and I'm all right too. Her marriage ended legally before mine. It was a rough period and she often thought she wouldn't make it through the proceedings without breaking down. But the divorce gave her a new way of looking at herself and it made her a role model for me. Observing how she was able to pick up the pieces of her new life was inspiring. Watching her make it was enough to convince me that I, too, had the ability to go through my emotional crisis and come out intact. Gloria's friendship and her strength have greatly assisted me in keeping my equilibrium and my sense of balance. Having her next door to provide warmth, love and support has been a comfort to me. It's usually easier to handle problems when there is someone with whom one can talk--someone who both empathizes and cares. Coping is decidedly easier for us both after we've had one of our late night talks. I suppose we're the kind of people who have a need to share our suffering and our pain. How fortunate that we can commiserate with each other. It is the dimension of our relationship--the being there when the other is in need--that has ultimately solidified our friendship and engendered mutual love and respect.

The ties which bind Gloria and me are deep. They have withstood the "causes celebres" of us both--the emergence of my black awareness and Gloria's feminism. During the height of the feminist movement she reprimanded me severely for my lack of participation and involvement. I, of course, protested strongly whenever she got on her soapbox. I never ceased to remind her that the world saw me as black first and then as a woman. My cause, therefore, was the black one. These differing points of view were responsible for many heated discussions between us. My black rage surfaced often during this period but Gloria never backed down nor did she change her opinion, and I never changed mine. It's fortunate for us both that we have enough love and respect for each other not to let our differences affect our relationship. Naturally we haven't resolved the issue of "Blackness vs. Feminism." But our discussions have developed into more lighthearted conversations.

The ease with which Gloria and I now communicate puts her into a special category. She is a loyal friend. She is someone with whom I am completely comfortable. I can be my total uncensored self when we're together. It's rare to find a person about whom one can say this. Gloria has soul. She feels, she is alive. Spending time together is never a strain because we compliment one another. We're both strong, dynamic women who are in the process of learning how to move more effectively through life. Discovering our relationship to the universe has become important to both of us. We constantly seem to be in the same space at the right time. Clearly, it was our sharing of pain and our mutual struggle to develop and to experience life which enabled us to transcend our racial, cultural and ethnic differences and to nurture our friendship.

ABOUT THE AUTHORS

ADAH ASKEW (Betty Bargonetti)
Administrator, counselor, educator--holds a Bachelor's degree in French and Italian, a Master's degree in Counselling, and has begun study for her doctorate in International Educational Development. Ms. Askew has worked for the Children's Television Workshop (Sesame Street) as an editor, writer, teacher and project developer, has performed Afro-Heritage dances under the direction of Pearl Primus, and is affiliated with the National Black Theatre of Harlem. Currently she works for a noted psychiatrist-Gestalt therapist and is involved in taking and teaching courses with the Arica Institute.

JAMES AXTELL
Professor of History at the College of William and Mary. He received his Ph.D. from Cambridge and has taught history at Yale and Sarah Lawrence. He recently spent two years as Research Fellow of the National Endowment for the Humanities, writing an ethnohistory of the colonial French, English and Indian efforts to convert each other. He has published many articles, papers and reviews in the field of colonial North American History, especially on Indian-white relations, and has done extensive editing of documentary sources. He is author of *The Educational Writings of John Locke, The School Upon a Hill: Education and Society in Colonial New England,* and (with James Ronda) *Indian Missions: A Critical Bibliography.*

RHODA GOLDSTEIN BLUMBERG
Who previously published under the name of Rhoda Goldstein, received her Ph.D. from the University of Chicago. A sociologist, she teaches race relations and formal organizations at Douglass College of Rutgers University, and is on the Graduate Faculty there. She was active in civil rights organizations in New Jersey and Chicago, and helped develop Afro-American Studies programs at Rutgers. She edited *Black Life and Culture in*

the United States and is author of *Indian Women in Transition: A Bangalore Case Study* (revised edition forthcoming), as well as articles and reviews in the fields of race relations, black studies and women's roles.

PRISCILLA READ CHENOWETH

Was a full-time mother and community activist for twelve years before returning to school to study law. She graduated from Rutgers-Newark Law School in 1968 and began practicing law that year. She is currently case digest editor of the New Jersey Law Journal. She was vice-chairwoman of Middlesex, New Jersey CORE, directed a civil rights radio program, and chaired her county Economic Opportunity Corporation. She currently serves on the Board of Trustees of the United Way of Central Jersey.

FRED CLOUD

Executive Director of the Metropolitan Human Relations Commission in Nashville, Tennessee and Adjunct Professor of Human Relations for the University of Oklahoma. He received the B.A. and M.Div. degrees from Vanderbilt University and an M.A. from Scarritt College. Mr. Cloud served as president of the National Association of Human Rights Workers in 1972-73 and as Vice chairman of the International Association of Official Human Rights Agencies in 1971-73. He has taught in this country, Central America, Europe, Asia and the South Pacific, and has written four books and numerous articles.

JOYCE A. LADNER

Professor of Sociology at Hunter College and received her Ph.D. from Washington University in St. Louis. She has been on the faculties of Southern Illinois and Howard Universities, was senior research fellow at the Institute of the Black World in Atlanta in 1969-70 and research fellow at the University of Dar-es-Salaam in Tanzania in 1970-71. She is author of *Tomorrow's Tomorrow: The Black Woman*, and editor of *The Death of White Sociology. Mixed Families,* a study of transracial adoption was published in 1977.

ELAINE PATRICIA McGIVERN

Is a doctoral candidate in the Department of Sociology, University of Pittsburgh. Her research interests include the effects of ethnic identification, ethnic group support systems, and status ranking processes within ethnic groups. Her dissertation, to be completed shortly, is a study of the persistence of ethnic identification among Irish Americans.

GLORIA FEMAN ORENSTEIN

Is Assistant Professor of English at Douglass College of Rutgers University, where she has also been the Acting Chairperson of the Women's Studies Program. She is the author of *The Theater of the Marvelous: Surrealism and The Contemporary Stage* and Contributing Editor of *Chrysalis* and *Womanart.* She has also published in *Signs, Heresies, Book Forum, Ms., Dada-Surrealism, The Feminist Art Journal* and *The Journal of Current Education.* She is the Co-Founder of the Woman's Salon in New York.

WENDELL JAMES ROYE

Is an Intergroup Relations specialist who has had a career in human relations at many levels, from street community organizing to graduate teaching. He is a past president of the National Association of Human Relations Workers. As Assistant Director of the National Center for Research and Information (NCRIEEO) at Teachers' College, Columbia, he developed programs to aid school desegregation. He was recently Director of the Regional Direction Center at CUNY and currently teaches at Plymouth State College in New Hampshire. His poetry appears in *Crisis* and in various anthologies and literary magazines.

JANET WARD SCHOFIELD

Received her doctoral degree in Social Psychology at Harvard, then served as research psychologist at the Office of Economic Opportunity and at the National Institute of Education. For the past several years, at the University of Pittsburgh, she has directed a research project on social processes in desegregated schools. Dr. Schofield has published numerous articles on the impact of school desegregation on the development of intergroup relations. Her other areas of interest include: the relationship between attitudes and behavior, children's friendship patterns, and research methodology.

WILLIAM SPINRAD

Is Professor of Sociology and co-ordinator of the Graduate Sociology Program at Adelphi University. Professor Spinrad has been particularly interested in public opinion, including its role in race relations. As a citizen he has participated in a variety of efforts to achieve and maintain integration since his undergraduate days at City College, New York in the late 1930's, and through the later civil rights struggles. A specialist in civil liberties, he has published *Civil Liberties,* articles and reviews, and is currently on the Board of Directors of the Nassau Country Civil Liberties Union.

C. HOYE STEELE

Is a Corrections Ombudsman in Virginia. A former teacher in Kansas (of Indians and non-Indians) and Virginia, he has also been a community organizer among low income blacks in Virginia and North Carolina. His Ph.D. degree was obtained from the University of Kansas. He is co-editor of *Majority and Minority: The Dynamics of Racial and Ethnic Relations* (revised ed., 1975), and is author of articles on Indian identity, ethnicity, and education.

JUNE A. TRUE

Received her Ph.D. at Rutgers University and is presently an assistant professor at Trenton State College, New Jersey. Dr. True was active in civil rights during the sixties, when her home in Plainfield, New Jersey was the meeting place for the local chapter of CORE. In 1972 she collaborated with Rhoda Goldstein (Blumberg) and Thomas Slaughter of Douglass College in a survey of Black Studies programs in four-year colleges in the United States. She has also published under the name of June True Albert.

GUIDA WEST

Is the Coordinator of Continuing Education for Women at Rutgers University. She was the recipient of a federally-funded grant to establish the Rutgers Training Institute for Sex Desegregation of the Public Schools. Dr. West was active in the civil rights movement, a charter member of a number of interracial groups in New Jersey, and also participated in the National Welfare Rights movement. Her doctoral dissertation was an analysis of the protest of welfare rights women from 1966-1976. Dr. West received her Ph.D. in political sociology from Rutgers and lectures on racism and sexism.

CHARLES VERT WILLIE

Distinguished Harvard sociologist, also well known in the field of religion. Formerly he was Vice-President for Student Affairs and Chairperson of the Department of Sociology at Syracuse University. He has served as President of the Eastern Sociological Society and on the President's Commission on Mental

Health. He is also a former Vice-President of the General Convention of the Episcopal Church in the United States. Among his publications are: *The Sociology of Urban Education, Black Colleges in America, A New Look at Black Families,* and *Racism and Mental Health.*

INDEX

Acculturation, 14-35
Adoption, by blacks, 169-170; Indian ceremonies of, 19-25; reforms in, 171; transracial, 8, 14-35, 153-174
Affirmative action, 69
Albert, June. *See* True, June
Alinsky, Saul, 73-74, 87
America, colonial, 11-35
Anthropologist, role of, 37-38, 43
Aptheker, Herbert, 3, 9
Askew, Adah, 8, 132
Attitudes, racial, 90, 92-93, 98-100, 107, 147-149. *See also* Prejudice
Axtell, James, 3, 10
Bennett, E.M. 143, 151
Bennett, Lerone, 135, 151
Black caucuses, 122-127
Black Panther Party, 72, 83-86
Black Peoples' Unity Movement ((BPUM), 72, 76-79
Black power movement, 5, 7, 53, development of coalitions in, 72-87; reasons for emergence of, 71
Blacks, and Jews, 175-190; as teachers of whites, 60; relations with police, 65, 68, 83-84; separatism of, 60-61, 124, 126-128, 167. *See also* Race relations
Black studies programs, 149
Blauner, Robert, 4, 9
Blumberg, Rhoda Goldstein, 149, 150
Bonds, interracial, nature of, 1-9
Boston, Massachusetts, twin-track coalitions in, 72, 79-83
Boston United Fund (BUF), 72, 79-83
Bouquet, Col. Henry, 14, 15, 16, 27, 29

Brickell, John, 33
Brink, William, 151
Cade, Toni, 135, 151
Camden, New Jersey, twin-track coalitions in, 72, 76-79
Carmichael, Stokely, 75, 79
Carter, Barbara, 87
Caucuses, black. *See* Black caucuses
Chambers, Ed, 73
Chaney, James, 5
Change, planned social, 63-70
Charlevoix, Pierre de, 21, 28
Chenoweth, Priscilla, 6, 52, 53
Children, adopted transracially, *see* Transracial adoption; adopted by Indians, treatment of, 29-32, 34. *See also* Adoption; in desegregated schools, 106-117
Civil rights laws. *See* legislation
Civil rights movement, 4-6, 52-53, 58-61, 177
Clashes, racial, 39, 65, 67, 73, 76, 77-79, 83-84, 122-126, 130
Cleaver, Eldridge, 83
Cloud, Fred, 6, 53
Coalitions, 40, 52, 53, 62-64, 67, 68; "twin-track", 5, 71-87
Cobbs, Price M., 135, 151
Cohen, Elizabeth G., 4, 9
Cohen, L.R., 143, 151
Colden, Cadwallader, 12-13
Colline, Mary, 98
Collins, Thomas, 106, 118
Comer, James, 165, 174
Congress of Racial Equality (CORE), 4, 52-54, 58-61
Council on Adoptable Children, 156, 171
Croghan, George, 19
Curtis, James L. 165, 172
Day, Beth, 135

De Beauvoir, Simone, 143, 146, 151
De Crevecoeur, Hector, 13, 34
De Gramont, Sanche, 87
Demonstrations, group, 49, 59, 62, 73, 76-79, 85
Desegregation, 6-7, 106-119. *See also* Integration
Deutsch, Helena, 136
Deutsch, Morton, 98
Dingwall, Eric, 139, 151
Discrimination, racial and religious, 38-39, 58-60, 64, 96, 158, 176-178; towards children, 158, 162-163; in employment, 58-60, 64, 96; structural factors, 88-105. *See also* Prejudice; Racism
Dollard, John, 134, 136, 151
Edgar, Margaret, 155, 156, 158-159, 172
Ellison, Ralph, 38
Episcopal Church, Hood conference of, 120-131
Falk, Lawrence, 172
Fanshel, David, 157-158, 172
Families, interracial. *See* Interracial
Fauquier, Lt. Governor, 15
Fernandez, John Peter, 82, 87
FIGHT, 72, 73-76
Fort Pitt, 14, 15
Fort William Henry, 20
Franklin, Benjamin, 13
Freedom Democratic Party, 4-5
Friendship, interracial. *See* Interracial
Friends of the Black Peoples' Unity Movement (BPUM), 72, 76-79
Friends of FIGHT, 72, 73-76
Friends of the Panthers, 72, 83-86
Fricke, Harriet, 155, 169, 172
The Fund for Negro Urban Development (FUND), 72, 79-83
Gage, General Thomas, 16
Goffman, Erving, 9

Goldstein, Rhoda L. *See* Rhoda Blumberg
Goodman, Andrew, 5
Grier, William H., 135, 151
Hagen, Clayton, 159-160, 173
Hamilton, Charles V., 87
Harris, Louis, 151
Hawryluk, Alexander, 87
Hill, Norman, 57-59
Hill, Robert, 170, 173
Hill, Velma, 57-59
Hoover, J. Edgar, 83
Horn, Marilyn, 173
Housing, as black power issue, 77; integrated, 97-104, 178; segregation in, 7
Human relations, commissions, 6, 53, 63-64; training in, 65
Identity, group, 107, 110-119; human, 128, 130-131, 159-162; Indian, by adopted whites, 15, 29-30, 34; racial or religious, 8, 11, 13, 41, 126, 156-157, 161-165, 178, 179, 181
Illich, Ivan, 69
Indians, acculturation practices of, 14-35; the Caughnewaga, 22,29; the Delawares, 14, 16, 25, 27, 33; the Iriquois, 23, 28; the Kickapoo, 36; the Pottawatomi, 36; the Senecas, 14, 20, 28; separatism of, 37-39, 41-42; the Shawnees, 14, 16, 25; stereotypes of, 38; urban, 36-51
Integration, in church groups, 121-131; conditions of successful, 7, 91-92, 100-101; definition of, 89-90; in employment, 95-97; goal of, 6; in housing, 97-104, 132; in the military, 94-95; oreo cookie as symbol of, 120; in public accomodations, 93; in sports, 91-92; in unions, 95-97
Interracial: cooperation, 49-50; dating, love and sexual relationships, 8, 14-16, 26, 56,

133-152; families, 156, 157, 162; friendships, 7, 8, 38, 56, 57, 61, 98-100, 132, 186-190; interaction disability, 4, 5, 7; interaction, situations of, 38, 50, 111-115; marriage, 16, 17, 26-27, 39, 121-131, 134, 136-137; relationships, secrecy about, 177. *See also* Race relations
Invisibility, of blacks, 60; of Indians, 38
Isolation, racial, 106
Jews, 55, 176-178. *See also* Blacks, and Jews
Johnson and Johnson corporation, 58-59, 61
Johnson, Sir William, 17, 29
King, Martin Luther, Jr., assassination of, 65, 77, 80, 83
Ladner, Joyce, 8, 132
Legislation, anti-discrimination, 61, 62, 64, 69, 71, 93
Lewin, Kurt, 64
Lincoln, Abby, 135, 151
Love, interracial. *See* Interracial; Race relations
McGivern, Elaine Patricia, 7, 88
Marriage, 16, 17, 26-27, 39, 121, 136-137, 143. *See also* Interracial marriage
Marx, Gary T., 5, 9
Massachusetts Council of Churches, Commission on Church and Race of, 79
Merton, Robert K. 137-139, 142, 146, 151
Minority Adoption Recruitment of Children's Homes (MARCH), 153-154
Myrdal, Gunnar, 140, 151
Narratives, captivity, 12-14, 35
Nashville, Tennessee, community coalitions in, 64-69
National Association for the Advancement of Colored People (NAACP), 56
National Association of Black Social Workers. *see* Social workers, black
Newby, Robert, 7, 9
Open Door Society (ODS), 155, 156, 166, 171
Open enrollment, 108
Orenstein, Gloria F., 8, 132
Organizations, movement. *See* name of organization
Noblit, George, 106, 118
Nutt, Thomas, 166-167, 173
Oliver, Peter, 33
Panunzio, Constantine, 136, 151
Parents to Adopt Minority Youngsters (PAMY), 155
Parsons, Talcott, 143, 146, 151
Pincus, Fred, 83, 86, 87
Police, relations with blacks, 65 68, 83-84
Prakash, Sethi S., 87
Prejudice, 55, 92, 104, 175, 177, 186-187; and Indians, 16, 22-24, 29, 30; sex differences in, 142, 147-149. *See also* Discrimination; Racism
Quarles, Benjamin, 5, 9
Race. *See also* Race relations; Racism; Interracial; and class, 84, 86, 108
Race relations, and anti-racist thought, 2-3; and churches, 73, 76, 78, 79, 120-131; Indian-black, 39, 49; Indian-Chicano, 39; Indian-white, 11-35, 36-51; and mass media, 66-68; in schools, 4, 106-118; spirit of love in, 128; teacher's role in, 109-113, 117. *See also* Interracial
Racism, 1-5; "reverse", 154, 168. *See also* Discrimination; Prejudice
Randolph, A. Philip, 57
Rape, attitude of Indians toward, 19
Raynor, Lois, 173
Reik, Theodore, 143, 152
Relationships, equal status, 8
Rochester, New York, twin-track coalitions in, 72, 73-76

Index

Roles, caretaker, 47; reversal of, 71-87; race and sex, 180; of women, 143-146
Rustin, Bayard, 56, 57, 62
Sanders, Marion K., 87
Schactman, Max, 57
Schaller, Lyle E., 65, 70
Schofield, Janet Ward, 7, 88
Schwerner, Michael, 5
Scyner, Lawrence A., 161, 173
Segregation, age, 121; racial, 55, 56. *See also* Separation, racial
Sellers, Cleveland, 8, 9
Separation, racial, 37-39, 41-42, 60-61, 124, 126-128, 167. *See also* Segregation
Sexual relationships, interracial. *See* Interracial dating, love and sexual relationships
Simon, Rita, 157, 173
Simpson, George E., 142, 152
Slaughter, Thomas, Jr., 149, 150
Smith, Rev. William, 15, 17, 18, 33
Snyder, John, 166-167, 173
Socialism, 55-57
Social workers, black, 153-154, 168-170, 172, 173
Sower, Christopher, 65, 66
Spinrad, William, 7, 88
St. Denis, Gerald, 173
Stearn, Gerald Emanuel, 87
Steele, C. Hoy, 3, 10, 51
Stein, Arthur, 9
Stember, Charles H. 140-141, 142, 144, 145, 152
Stereotypes, of blacks, 39, 170; of Indians, 38; racial, among children, 107
Surrealist movement, 185
Suzuki, Ryo, 173
Tajfel, Henri, 107
Terrell, Robert, 8, 9
Tillich, Paul, 120, 131
Transracial adoption; defense of, 153, 159, 162, 165, 166, 168; issues in 154, 156-158, 160; opposition to, 153, 156-157; studies of, 157-159
True, June, 5, 8, 132, 150
Twin-track coalitions, in Baltimore, 83-86; in Boston, 79-83; in Camden, 76-79; principles of 72, 86; in Rochester, 72, 73-76
U.S. Civil Rights Commission, 93
Useem, Michael, 5, 9
Values, Indian, 18-20, 33, 40-41, 44
Walton, William, 32
Wax, Rosalie, 43
Weisbord, Robert G., 9
Welfare rights, coalition groups for, 53
West, Guida, 5, 53
White, Herbert, 73
Williams, Bill, 58, 62
Williams, Rev. John, 27, 30
Williams, Robin M., Jr., 2, 9
Williams, Roger, 33
Willie, Charles V., 3, 8, 88
Women, aspirations and motives of, 144-146, 178; identity as vs. racial identity, 181, 182, 189; sexuality of, 140-142, 145; white, and black men, 133-152; white, degree of prejudice of, 142, 147-149; white, treatment of by Indians, 18-33
Workshops, in non-violence, 78
Yinger, J. Milton, 142, 152